AF572326

PROBING MINDS

SALAMANDER GIRLS

A DOG NAMED SALLY

Probing Minds Salamander Girls & A Dog Named Sally

A Hubbard Mountain Memoir by

HARRISON WRIGHT

GASPEREAU PRESS
Printers & Publishers
2005

To the Wrights, to the MacInnis clan, to Pereaux and area, to Jeremy Parent, who said one night after some reminiscing and a couple of beers, "Hey, you know what you should do? Write some stories about some of these times.... " Smiling at the idea and thinking maybe I had had too many Keith's myself because it didn't seem half bad, "Nah," I replied, "What do I know? I wouldn't know how to go about it really," and I still don't. But early the next morning one thing led to another and I began writing. And finally to Ron MacInnis who saw something in these stories and figured others may too.

FOREWORD *13*

1 *Coming Home* *25*

2 *Hairiness on a Moped* *31*

3 *Jer, the Summer, Living & Working, Working & Living* *41*

4 *Aerial Runway* *59*

5 *The Basement* *71*

6 *Barebone, Moonlit Wonder* *83*

7 *Fateful Zucchini* *93*

8 *There's Only One Fishing Story* *103*

9 *Old Maples* *115*

10 *The Trick* *127*

11 *Farewell, Pheasant* *141*

12 *The Bizarre Particulars of a Day (& a Dried-Up Frog)* *167*

13 *We Went, We Came Back, It's Something You Do* *175*

14 *On Thin Ice with the Moped* 195

15 *Feels Like You're Doin' Somethin'* 207

16 *Green Fields & Pink Skies* 219

17 *Fargos, Salamander Girls, Probing Minds & Fires (A great story becomes bewilderingly short & possibly not so great)* 225

AFTERWORD 245

Foreword

Make yourself comfortable, have a seat. This is not your conventional style of book, and so, I think given the sort it is, the foreword becomes that much more important. So cross your legs, recline your chair, do that thing where you tuck your hand into your pants, whatever it is you do when making yourself comfortable. I must urge you to resist the temptation to flip by this foreword so as to shorten the amount of time the reading of this book will consume. I know you are tempted to do this because I myself, I shamefully admit, do the exact same thing more often than not.

When I start into a book I usually believe that the author's beliefs or designs can't be half so interesting or clever as my own, so their words only deserve my divided attention. Then, somewhere between the twenty and the thirty page mark, I find my pace slowing and the time in the world's continuum along with it. Some anticipated task becomes gradually not so important, and I forget about time—I live for a while without even thinking about it, which is the only way you can. I have to say I am cautious in suggesting that this may occur in the reading of *this* book, but you may 's well give her a go. If you are rather rushed, have a hectic schedule, or are now wondering what is on Fox later tonight, you might as well put this book back on the shelf from whence you got it, let the dust collect on these thoughts and adventures once more, or return it to the owner of the window out of which it flew just moments ago, only to land at your feet, you merely opening it to the first page so as to satiate your curiosity as to the grounds for such an act—another busy soul.

As I write this, the air is rather still in here, and I do believe my collar is a little tight. What the hell, I'll take my shirt right off, for what's the difference? I admit right now I am eyeing my own window in a most designing manner … ah, there we go, a little air in here should do me good. I think I need a little oxygen in my brain, for I do not always think so clear and I have trouble being clever. And so bear with me, because this book is meant as a getaway from the introduction-skipping mentality.

It seems to me that people—myself included, for that is how I really know—often defer their life to that better time in the future, the time they are working for, that job they don't enjoy so much, the time they unquestionably sacrifice their current lives for, possibly hoping for the day when their lives will better resemble those that are portrayed in movies: the ideal, a large house, a car whose name you mostly pay for, money streaming out of every orifice, kids (at least two, they'll amuse each other), drama, action, a purpose that is understandable, makes sense, is aesthetically pleasing, a closet with a time-saving 'Swiffer' in it. These ideals are propped up for us—most of them available on E-bay, you with your credit card number ready—and people assume they should strive for them and be happy with them because they suppose their neighbours are doing so. Everybody scrambling, dogging it, and trying to put down payments on the life they wish to obtain.

This book shows time. I have tried to clear my head (at least for a while) of these ideals which we are asked to strive for, the ones that drive economies, as though a raging economy, the flow of money quickly to all corners, is the be-all and end-all. Marketing tries to sell us things to save us time; presidents, prime ministers and politicians often think about time in four-year blocks; time is relative; if time were really infinite there could be no beginning and no today; time … a point, a point, a thing to grasp onto with relief, one should be in every paragraph.… These stories are about living and about the passage of time when the characters weren't too sure how it was they were supposed to go about living, and hadn't heard, or at least hadn't paid attention to, any presidential or prime ministerial addresses telling them how to "spend" their time, and so they tried figuring out how to go about things on their own—like apple trees in the middle of the woods growing wildly up, out, and all over the place, not knowing they are only supposed to be seven-feet tall and shaped like Christmas trees, growing only in rows by the thousands. This book is about making do with the present. It is about the simple passage of time and the events therein, the simple beauty in life that should be within everybody's means.

I will go over a few of the more prominent characters in the book—and I should mention it now, if I have not already, that these are all real people and the stories are all real stories, and by *real,* I mean, this is me saying what I think happened, before you get on my case. They made them wiry out there in Pereaux; maybe it was something in the water, I don't know. We all thought we were smarter than your average bears, even if it was in that way that doesn't necessarily show in school, and that still allows for a major blunder every now and again. I often wonder if most sort of feel this way, and if that is what that little spark in the eye of so many people is. Sometimes even a person without a roof, whose pants are worn through and so wears two pairs and hopes the holes don't match up, and who never got beyond the number of grades he can count on his one hand, even if he had all his fingers, has this spark and he looks out at people passing by and thinks, "Ha, fools," with a little smile and a slight shake of his head. But not fools in a bad or malicious way—just fools in that they seem to be missing that thing he thinks he knows: couldn't say exactly what it is, or would become exasperated when he sets out to do so, but is glad he knows it anyway. So we all thought we were smart is what I'm getting at.

Paul MacInnis is the oldest MacInnis brother. A year older than me, and hence sophisticated: good diction (except for that time we all replaced sixty percent of our vocabulary with the words "bink" and "bonk," in an effort to simplify things). Scott MacInnis is a year younger than me: mechanical, resourceful, entrepreneurial, an individual and the sort that would lead you down a path like he knew the way even if he had never been there before. And Matt MacInnis is the youngest, but not the least mature: clever, three years younger than Scott, yet he always seemed our age. He would always be one of the first to crack a joke, and everyone would want him to. We always thought he must have got his humour from us, growing up, until it seemed like he was funnier than we were. Jeremy Parent, or Jer, is the same age as me. He is another friend of ours and you will find he saunters in and out of many of the stories. Tall, the son of a preacher man (later the MLA), and for a while at parties he even had his own theme song, sung by none other than Aretha Franklin. Me? You'll have to ask around. Ron is the MacInnis boys' father; they have a mother of course, Carole; there's Dale, Eben, Kelly and others kicking around; I have parents, a brother and sisters; there are crickets I guess and frogs, the salamander girls, a neighbour's dog named Sally, and hell, I'm trying to speed this along, there are others as well, but let them establish themselves in due course, because all this formality is starting to get to me, and I can only carry on in such a fashion for so long I find. In my head as I name each person I can almost picture them standing up and stepping forward, maybe giving a little bow with a nervous smile, the sort where you can feel your smile muscles, and maybe giving me a look because it all seems a little forced. I know that the people I name, unless playing themselves, would not make much in the way of actors in such a charade, but wonderful characters, and so let's let everyone just sit down again and not forget ourselves; this was my fault. The ages of some of the main characters will vary with the years from around fourteen to twenty-four and older. (But let's not get too caught up in age while reading. I knew things at twenty-four that I never would have known at fourteen, but at fourteen I knew things that were destined to be forgotten by twenty-four.) The seasons vary from summer to winter, the time from day to night, and the mood from happy and content to depressed and uncertain, from sure to unsure.

You're probably still wondering what you're getting into here; I guess I'll try to explain a little more. It's a good thing I am writing or I would undoubtedly stumble over a few words and let my voice trail off into a quiet muttering as I walked away, pretending I had to be somewhere, hoping you had heard something I didn't say, because I needed more time to collect my thoughts, or rather to corner them. I picture the process of cornering a good thought as being like catching a chicken: the people who come along when a barn of chickens is being emptied who are in charge of catching the stragglers, sometimes slipping and sliding around. Fiddle music would be coming from somewhere I suppose.... A thought, a good thought, can be just as elusive or as hard to pin down as a feisty chicken. If you are smart you know you have to let it come to you.

I guess these words will be about me, growing older and trying to gain a degree of understanding about the world, if there can be such a thing. I started writing to remember where I came from and to think about where I am going, and I figured by drawing a mean between the two I might get a sense of where I am. This is all probably starting to sound a little hokey and out there, and I know, I don't like that "out there" stuff myself. There is nothing worse than sitting there, hearing someone go on, unwilling to get sucked into their senseless ramblings and growing tired of staring at their eyebrows. So I will try and keep all my "out there" stuff to a bare minimum.

I hope this book to be about words—and not just words, but language, for the human language is the medium that we take in and shape the world with, what we find ourselves in. I don't just mean the *English* language in its most elite form, where some people will take two or three words and turn them into one word that few have heard of, as though it were a code or a secret, but the language of the body, the eyes, a nod of the head, a look down at the ground, the unspoken understandings when someone says "I can't figure ..." or "I wouldn't much know ..." and then goes on to tell you what they think they know or figure, the first words only a quick cover, something to fall back on in case you don't agree with them.

That said, this book does not contain much more sex or violence than is generally found in the lives of those who sleepily get their mail in their pajamas, with their rubber boots on because these are easy to slip into in the morning, which can still be a lot, or those who wipe their nose on their sleeve when they think no one is looking. And there is no more cursing than is generally heard—most often from a stubbed toe or in reaction to a piece of equipment that's been broken, or just right out of nowhere when you get a little excited about something and your usual words fail you for a second. It is a collection of stories, just as all lives are collections of stories. In life there is not necessarily a climax, a grand finale, or symbolism in every object. When you focus on the details, the overall structure of life is sometimes lost, and maybe this is not so bad. This is not a tragedy or a comedy, the ending will not necessarily be punctuated with a wedding or a funeral, no scripts or protocols are followed, things simply are.

I don't want this to read like a group of unconnected short stories, however, like a mess of people in the city waiting for the light at a crosswalk. These stories are all set in rural Pereaux, Nova Scotia, for the most part on a small winding dirt road called the Hubbard Mountain, with a "No Exit" sign at the end of it, situated right underneath the North Mountain, not far from the Minas Basin. The fringe of the earth to a lot of people I suppose, but it is dead centre to most of the people who live there. In these stories things will happen, stuff will be said, and there'll be people coming and going. Sometimes they may leave a name or sometimes the writing may be more in the spirit of saying, "Now who was that that just went down the road?" and getting up to look out the window, and somebody else says, "Someone driving a blue truck. Who do we know with a blue truck?" and nobody knows anyone with a blue truck and the issue is forced to be left at that and if you know what's best you move on and don't dwell on it too long like some are inclined to.

This is sort of a memoir—maybe nowhere near complete, but which ones are? To ask for too much reasoning, structure and consistency would be asking me to sometimes lie, for those things are not always on hand and cannot always be found in life, I find. You should think of it as being like when someone is telling a story about the other day, and they are just telling it like it is, and they are just getting to the part they wanted to get to, and the thing is going good and they are working themselves up and they say, "and I says to the guy, I says … and well wouldn't you know it, but just around the time Ian Janes walked in the door … I happened to look out the window and, haha (knee slapping) here, down the way, comes this great big …" and right there the teller is cut off because someone sees fit to say, "Whoa now, who the hell is this Ian Janes feller anyway?" And even though Ian Janes is Ian Janes and he is sure to have a story of his own, right then is not the time for it. The teller was just telling you how it happened his own way, which may be the most important thing to pay attention to, and now he has to answer your question—maybe he doesn't know, or you've messed him up—others are looking at you, and either the teller can't remember where he was or he doesn't even feel like telling you what was coming anymore. No one wants to be that someone.

Finally—and I'm winding down here, if you're glancing at the clock or just gave a slight sigh—I am not just embarking on the writing of this thing in the same way you are when reading it, so please feel no journey-embarking-compatriotism with me, for as you are reading this I am undoubtedly standing around with my hands in my pockets periodically going down on one knee to pull up my sock, even though it may be completely unnecessary—but one mustn't appear idle, for someone who appears idle must be thinking, and that tends to make people nervous I find. Or maybe I am glancing at my shoes or the state of the backs of my hands, so as to appear engrossed in something and therefore too busy to notice any chary looks I may receive from passersby.

I already do not like what I just said, for even though the standing around scenario is probably not far from the truth, the old romantic notion of the reader embarking on a journey with the writer is a rather enchanting one, which I hold dear.

I'm just thinking on my feet here, but I guess by reading what I have written you will be, in some faint sort of way, embarking on the same journey that I have, and you can think of me as merely waiting for you, in a most eager and impatient way, at the end of the road, so that you and I can both carry on excitedly about what wc have seen and heard and somewhat mutually experienced, or at least caught wind of, like a couple of swallows, up on the wire ... by the barn, twittering away, and whose superior level they feel puts them in the right of soiling the tops of the heads of anyone who passes under them. Yeah, the reading of a book should be thought of just like that. I do not believe the concept of the reader-writer relationship has ever before been put so eloquently. What I write is a part of me, and is a part of me still. And I guess since they are memories which I constantly relive, the old romantic idea is not so far off as I first thought. So let us pretend I said nothing on the matter and let's not mention another word about it, except for the swallow thing perhaps, which I think I might bring up a few more times, possibly at parties with a beer in one hand while my other is wildly gesturing in my attempt to fully bring home the meaning of the swallow to whoever my listener may be. And if I am delusional enough to think that I have possibly planted another seed of wisdom in the world which will undoubtedly spread throughout and flourish, affecting many others, even if only faintly, like the dandelions on my front lawn or the red sock in my wash, then let me be, for it is harmless enough.

All right, you have been most patient and understanding through this all. Let me finally introduce you to this book, for that is what this foreword is: a bit of a warming up, an introduction of a sort, a setting of the scene, a drink to be social—a gaining of acquaintance of strangers.

And so, this is a piece of my thoughts, my memories, my little world, insignificant and one of many, as charming as a dog trying to sniff your crotch, as flashy as an '81 Corolla hatchback with a hole in the manifold, as romantic as two skunks in a culvert and you with a grin and a hose, but as real as real can really be, to me, and as best as I can possibly express it, to you.

1 *Coming Home*

Paul was expected to return that day from the Yukon, where he had been on a student exchange program with the school for some time. Everybody's heart was full in anticipation of the mirth and festivities that were sure to be had a little later on after everything had calmed down. It was that time of year in between late spring and early summer. That time of year when you really appreciate the sun, the flowers and all the green foliage the most, because it all seems so new again after the long months of winter and the cold grey wet spring we always seemed to have, each one seeming colder and wetter than the last (this said less about the weather than about how quickly we'd forget). It was just after supper, and the day was still warm and bright, though the shadows were becoming long and drawn out. Matt and myself were wandering about the lawn aimlessly, really not doing a whole lot more than the couple of stray bunnies that were hopping around. In fact, we were probably even doing less than the bunnies, because even the bunnies nibbled on the grass or some clover every once in a while. It is hard for me to comprehend now what it was like to have so little to do.

Scott was busy preparing for Paul's return as Matt and I puttered about. Scott had acquired himself a number of lawn mowers and whipper-snippers in Paul's absence. Scott was quite proud of his mowers. He was going into the mowing business. He had a good head for working on things, and he enjoyed going around to yard sales, junkyards and other laudable places to find deals. We all were like that I guess. Scott, however, was particularly into lawn mowers at this point in time. When Scott got into something he went full tilt. In anticipation of Paul's rapidly approaching arrival, he had hauled his equipment out of the old barn where he stored all of his treasure. I believe he had three or four push mowers, and I know he had three whipper-snippers. He lined the three whipper-snippers up along the porch railing so they would be the first things anyone would see when they pulled up the driveway. The mowers he parked out in front of the porch. Matt and I figured if he took the parts that were any good off all his equipment he might have one good working lawn mower, and one, one-and-a-half good working whipper-snippers. Occasionally Matt and I would glance over to see what he was doing, making some quip to Scott that we would all laugh at. Something along the lines of "Hey, what's Winker up to over there?" or "Having some problems with your cutter?" Matt and I both thought we were particularly witty, even if it was the type of humour where you had to be there, or you had to know the person. Everybody around there had a pretty good sense of humour really.

The time finally came; we heard one of the old Toyotas trying to make its way up the long dug-out sandy hill that was the driveway. The driveway seemed more like a tunnel than a driveway when you drove up it. The banks on either side towered ten or twelve feet above the car in spots. You couldn't even see a car coming from the huge old house until it reached the top of the hill where the house was situated. There, the sandy banks gave away to the slight grassy slope of the MacInnises' lawn, and then to the parking spot across from the house. You got to know the engines of the different cars, and we knew this was Paul coming up now. Paul parked the car, got out, and approached the house with his big duffle bag in hand. Ron came out of the house slowly and walked along, across the lawn, as though out for a stroll. Matt and I did not run over, but we meandered a little closer to the house so we could hear anything Paul had to say to his father about his trip. Scott looked up a second and then stepped up the pace of the work he was doing on one of the whipper-snippers. Apparently he was almost done. Ron and Paul were talking away, going about the usual pleasantries you do when you first see someone you haven't seen for a long time. They were still talking when Scott got his whipper-snipper back together and brought it over to about ten feet from where they were standing. Scott had a proud smile on his face. He looked up and grinned at Paul a moment and then, without having said a word to his brother, turned his attention back to the whipper-snipper and gave the rip cord a pull. The thing started right up. Ron and Paul still tried to talk for a short bit, but it was hard with Scott right there, revving the small whiny engine on the whipper-snipper up and down. I'm pretty sure this was Scott's own special way of greeting Paul back. He wasn't trying to drown them out, but he was quite proud of his mowers; he was showing his brother what he had done, probably better than words would have. After revving the engine up and down several times, he set about mowing a bit of grass around one of the flower beds that really did not need mowing. It was only a few feet from where Ron and Paul were standing. They had stopped talking by this time; the only sounds now in the twilight of that warm day were the whine of Scott's whipper-snipper and the muffled chuckles of Matt and myself. We were now only a few paces away from Paul and Ron too, as though the whipper-snipper and Scott's shenanigans were bringing us all together. Paul waited just long enough, and then, talking over the noise of the small engine, asked Scott to turn off the machine for a moment. Scott, feigning like he supposed he could stop his important work a second, turned the engine off and came over and shook Paul's hand with a strong grip, his other hand still tightly clasping the whipper-snipper. Matt and I were still a little cautious. Paul was the oldest of any of us. Now that he had been gone for a couple of months we weren't really sure if we were dealing with a man, or what he was. Maybe he had gotten to know some distant equivalent of a salamander girl. We really did not know what to say to him if he was a man; time had passed.

Then Paul said, "What are you two yokels standin' there starin' at?"

And that was all we really needed. Maybe Paul had not become a man, or maybe there was a little bit more man in all of us. Or maybe none of us really gave much weight or credence to what this whole being a man business entailed. Either way, it was a good day. We all sauntered back to the porch. It looked out to where the sun was setting, not another house in sight, the North Mountain stretching westwards, you could watch a rainstorm come down along its ridge from hours away. Ron sat in one of the chairs, and Paul sat in another one, kind of like he'd earned it that day for going and coming back. Scott just leaned against the post and looked out over the fields with a somewhat nostalgic look upon his face, appreciating what was before him, seemingly, years ahead of his time. Matt and I sat on the step and lazily flicked the rocks that were about our feet. Ron was asking Paul questions. Paul was glad to be back, and everybody was glad to have him back. Although none of us really looked like it, Paul had our absolute attention. We all just sat there completely soaking up the moment. It was good that Paul was back. There would be time later for us all to put our heads together to see what we wanted to do. We too had our stories that Paul would need to know, and Paul would tell us his stories in his own way and time. Later, plans would be made to make new stories.

2 *Hairiness on a Moped*

It was another one of those hot lazy summer evenings. The trees cast long shadows in the setting sun. The lighting gave you an almost surreal feeling. If it wasn't for the crickets chirping, I don't know, but I might still find myself lost in that dream. Matt, Scott and I were lounging about the porch just watching the sunset, and waiting for the time to pass. There wasn't much to be said that evening. We had said everything we needed to say earlier. There had been plenty of jokes and laughing. Now we were just sitting there waiting for the MacInnises' mother, Carole, to get back with the Corolla, so we could convince her to take us to the Pereaux store to rent a movie and get some penny candy. That was all it really took to satisfy us back then.

 If on any given day, occasionally after coming into a little bit of money from some small job we'd done, we could get some candy and a movie, then it was deemed a very good day by all.

"You know, I got the moped going earlier ..." Scott said offhandedly. Sort of like a question, but the question wasn't whether we knew this fact or not, it was what we all thought now that we knew.

"That's the sort of thing you should have mentioned quite a long time ago," Matt said, after a pause, with a straight face. The excitement in all of us built. We talked about what our new options were, and fed off each other's excitement. Scott knew that we would have wanted to know about the moped, and that was why he had waited. Obviously he had not been as bored as we were the whole time we were sitting there waiting on the porch, because he was anticipating the excitement we were going to have. He knew that waiting would only make it better. Scott knew things like that. Some people might have run around flapping their arms, alerting the whole world when they had fixed a moped; but Scott, he knew it would be best to drop it on us like that when the time was just right, when we weren't expecting it.

None of us forgot about waiting for the MacInnises' mom, or going to the store, but now it was obvious that this was something we would have to do first. It was almost as though we were going to be driving the moped partway to the store ourselves. (Scott and I had already tried that.) Even though we would not be driving the moped in the direction of the store, and in all likelihood would be driving it over jumps and in circles and in no direction in particular, it still nonetheless seemed as though, to get to the store, some of the passage of the rest of the day would have to involve the moped. The ultimate destination of the journey was still the Pereaux store.

Now that our path was keenly understood, we were eager to embark. After a little more discussion we got up and sauntered over to the barn. I noticed there was a little more spring in all of our steps, now that we knew what we were all put here on this earth for (at least for that particular day). We knew that we were to ride the moped for a time, until we noticed the MacInnises' mom was back, and then we would convince her to take us to the store. Later we would enjoy a movie and some penny candy upstairs on the big bed. Scott and I went into the barn to fish the moped out, and Matt went around to the back to unhook the bigger door, where the ramp to roll the thing out of the barn was. The bike was an extremely old, sixties vintage, fifty-cubic-centimetre engine moped. It got well over a hundred miles per gallon, which was something we could appreciate and Mother Nature could too. Scott and I pushed that moped out of the barn with the same pride and determined resolve that you might see on the faces of a race crew as they pushed their prized vehicle out into the cheering crowd, although our only crowd was Matt, and he wasn't cheering. He just stood there staring at us with a small, knowing, sarcastic smile on his face. "You guys get lost in there or something? What took you so long?"

At first we took turns driving about the field. While one of us drove, the other two would chase him, throwing various things at him, or just trying to catch him. We would do this until we got tired and then we would sit down. The guy on the moped would continue to drive around the field. It would remain this way until the guy on the moped would try and hit the two sitting on the ground, or until the guy on the moped offered someone else a turn. The grassy field eventually got boring and we decided we should drive on over to the gravel pits to see what sort of excitement they had to offer a few young boys. We decided it was not too much to ask of the moped to carry all three of us, so we piled on. Scott was the driver, and Matt and I tried to make the best of the carriage rack on the back. It was a little much for the moped, but it was still amazing the way it carried us along. The only difference we could see in the moped with all of us on it was that it was a little slower going up the hills and it was faster and more out of control going down. We really felt we had it together with that moped.

We finally made it to the gravel pits. We pulled up to the very edge of one of the sandy cliffs. The cliffs were probably around seventy or eighty feet tall, with a very steep grade. Around the perimeter at the top, the grass held the dirt together; the sand below it had eroded, however, causing a large overhang. The sun was just ducking down under the horizon by this time and the view was really something. Naturally, being three boys so free in such a beautiful setting, we all walked up to the very edge and pissed out over it. We enjoyed seeing how far it had to go before it hit the ground. It's hard to explain why that feeling is so great, but it just is. I'd recommend pissing off a cliff to anybody. Few'll do it, though. You have to use your imagination a little. People sometimes, I don't know.

We lounged about at the top of the pit for a little bit as the sun slipped away. Mostly we were just talking, looking, and throwing the occasional clump of dirt over the edge to watch it explode at the base of the pit. It was just us at the pit; it was just us for miles and miles. Finally we decided we should head down in, for not much more reason other than we could. On the other side of the pit there was a road that crossed a little creek and headed into the pit on a more level piece. We would have to travel all the way around the pit to get in that way. From where we were the best route was a pretty steep and rough road that went down into the pit. A bulldozer had carved the route years before. The rain had carved huge crevasses down the wheel tracks, making the route impassable to the novice moped drivers. Luckily, none of us considered ourselves novice moped drivers. We all piled on the moped again and headed on down the track.

By this time it was starting to get dark. The track was even rougher than we had first perceived. The little bike started picking up more and more speed as we careened down the embankment. Scott was doing a commendable job of staying out of the ruts and keeping the bike upright, but we were going faster and faster and the ride was getting rougher and rougher. It was impossible to slow the bike down. We knew that things were getting dire, and we knew there was only so much we could do to stop them from becoming more so. There wasn't much panic in any of us; we were all completely aware of what was going on and the situation we were in. If there was a change in our demeanours it may have been that our eyes were all just a little bit wider than they had been at the top of the hill. There were no screams or yells, and no one grabbed at one another with a frenzied grip. That just was not the sort of people we were. You can lose that instinct after a while if you've a mind to, and in time you learn you're better off. We were just sitting there thinking, and readying ourselves for whatever was about to befall us.

Finally, what we all knew would happen happened. The moped's skinny front tire caught and twisted in one of the grooves in the steep road. The little bike went ass over teakettle sending us all flying. For a while we kept on travelling down the hill at approximately the same speed. It was just a tumble of bodies and mopeds going down the hill. We were all flying over each other; the bike was flying around, sometimes landing on us, sometimes us landing on it. Time stretched out and it seemed long, but it was probably only a few seconds. Inevitably, like all good and bad things, the tumult came to an end. We all sat there in a bit of a daze for a couple minutes, bewildered from all the rattling. We were bruised and scraped up some, but none of us was really hurt, and none of us was sorry we had done it. We were just as good as those Timex watches people are always talking about; we could take quite a lickin'. The moped was on its side still running strong. Somehow in the crash the throttle had gotten itself stuck wide open. The engine was burning hot, and because of the stress it was under it kept letting out these thunderous backfires that shot blue flames a couple feet into the air. Gas had somehow spilled all over the bike. All of us started to run for it, but as we were doing so, the moped, it blew up. One of the backfires, or maybe just the heat from the engine, ignited the gas that was lying all around. It lit up in a second, and the flame was everywhere. That caused us all to hesitate and re-evaluate the situation. Then we all started throwing and kicking dirt on the little bike. I felt bad throwing all that dirt on the moped, which had always been so good to us and had provided us with so many good times. I could only hope it understood that we were doing this for its own good. We started to worry that maybe the worst had not yet come. The flames were licking the moped's gas tank, and the cap was still on so we knew it was probably under some pressure. It seemed like it could be a little dangerous. Matt and I decided we would take off, and we started running for the sandy hills, ran like something was chasing us; we ran up the hills as far as we could. We turned around and sat in the sand on the slope to watch Scott put out the last of the flames. All of us had been a little scared of the flames, but that was not entirely why Matt and I had run. It just feels good to run away from something like that sometimes. Most people are always so safe these days; they don't know what it feels like to run away from a flaming moped. The things most people run away from are more complicated. They run away from things like deadlines, commitments and other more abstract dangers. The danger Matt and I were running away from was a type of danger that is easily perceived and has been built into us all since the beginning of time.

 These are things everybody can understand. Hardly anyone ever faces or cares about these dangers in life anymore; that is why it felt so good that Scott, Matt and I still had them; simple uncomplicated dangers. They trigger some primal mechanism that we all like to have triggered, at least once in a while. I imagine those crazy few who decide to run from the bulls in Spain know what I am talking about, but most would shake their head.

Matt and I climbed back down the slope and walked over to Scott, chuckling with each other. We all stood and looked down upon the moped. We all had little smiles on our faces and were enjoying the effects of the adrenaline still in our systems. "Thanks for taking off like that," Scott grinned at us. We figured Scott'd had it under control. It was now practically nighttime; it was pretty well completely dark. Even if you had just arrived on the scene you would have known from the feeling in the air that it had not been dark for very long. There is just this feeling like that in the air, I find. You can't pinpoint it, but there is still some residue of the life that resided in the day hanging around. Of course there is a new life that develops in the night, a mysterious dark life.

We were all still standing around and inspecting the moped when we heard a sound. An Aurora or maybe it was a Hercules flew slowly over. It was a huge four-engine military plane. They flew out of Greenwood, a military base probably fifty miles or so to the west. It was flying right over us and extremely low. It had a whole lot of bright lights on all over it: searchlights, and coloured flashing ones that helped it land and let you know its orientation in the sky. It was most likely on a search and rescue mission. They did that sometimes when a boat got in trouble off the shore from us, or when someone was lost or in danger somewhere unknown—maybe out there alone in a world that thinks little of dying, seemingly forgotten. For a second that was scarier than the moped. For a moment in our confused states we all thought that maybe the plane had something to do with us, that we were who it was looking for—but of course it flew right on over and by. With its passing our thoughts that we were somehow its cause went too. People, their actions, a smile, a whimper, can be so easily lost and go unnoticed in the remote corners of this world. I hoped whoever the search plane was looking for was alright. We were alright.

3 *Jer, the Summer, Living & Working, Working & Living*

This will not so much be a story of the conventional sort where you can point to the beginning, the middle and then the end, in the same way that a doctor can easily point out the parts of the body, possibly even naming them in Latin, on a diagram, or that a mechanic can point out the various devices, workings, and implements under the hood of your car. No, this will not be like that. I don't know what this will be, to tell you the truth, now that I have sat down and thought about it, but give me a minute to let me think some more, and I will see … I guess it will be more like a pondering, or a reflecting of times, or better yet of *a* time. Maybe you could refer to it as a number of stories all rolled into one. No one of them will be fully complete, but all together they offer themselves the semblance of some sort of conglomerate that will create a type of whole. That was rather clumsy I'm afraid.... I must better explain myself. It will be the sort of thing that is often created and recounted when you are sitting with friends, out on a deck, watching the sun wane, with a beer in your hand, resting it on the arm of your chair, possibly after a long day of labour. As you and your friends look out at the sun, you see nothing directly in front of you, or in the immediate vicinity, that calls for any commenting on. Maybe you have sat there with the same friends in the same manner many times before, and everything in your radius of vision has already been commented on many times over in evenings past. Maybe the day has been long as well, and much has already been said, so for now you all just sit enjoying your beers and thinking, analyzing your own thoughts. This silence stretches and the minutes slip past because no one has hit upon anything that they think is important enough to open their mouths for; nothing yet that could warrant such an effort on such a warm sunny evening, with the beer tasting more refreshing than it does in the house or at a bar, somehow mixing with the fresh air; nothing yet that could warrant disturbing the soothing silence. As you continue to reflect, after you have already jumped around between the ideas and the thoughts of the goings-on of that particular day and your immediate surroundings, your mind begins to wander backwards in time in search of something that is worth breaking the silence for, searching. Finally, just when you are on the verge of thinking that you will be utterly lost in your personal thoughts—maybe struggling with some elusive dilemma of the mind, taken away from the closeness of your friends for a time—some fond though jumbled memories come back to you. Not a story really, but definitely something worth professing out loud, you believe, something of interest. You glance around a second to see what state everybody else is in, to see if they look as if they are ready to hear someone speak, to see if they look as though they will be accepting of this breaking of the silence. Maybe one of your friends seems lost in the sky for a second, another in mid-sip of her beer, still another looks as though he is busy peeling the label off his bottle. You will give them a moment you decide, a moment more for you to go over what you are about to say, to get it as straight as you can in your head, and to continue to remember the times for yourself, smiling at your memories and at what you are about to say. It hits you that it is the time. Some people are starting to look restless; you can tell that although the silence had its time, it has now been too long. The floor is yours, and so you begin. "I remember the time when I was back in … when I used to…." That is what this is, one of those, and so let me now begin, and please continue to sip your beer at intervals if you like, for at intervals with a pleasant scape laid out before you, to help conjure your thoughts, is when beer is at its best—and I can most assure you that I will have a couple sips of mine as well, undoubtedly going through a few beers before I am done, sometimes getting up to go to the fridge to get another, but starting up where I left off as soon as I get back.

I remember back when I worked on the family farm with my friend Jer, we used to roam the hills. Jer is a tall, six-foot-four, lanky fellow with whom I have often shared a few beers, sometimes in the very manner I have just portrayed. We share each other's sense of humour pretty well, and with a good sense of humour you can say just about anything you like to another person who shares it. When everything can be said you can be pretty good friends—and so Jer was a pretty good friend, and still is I might add. Jer had not grown up on a farm as I had. I had always prided myself on working hard and on being as strong as an ox. Jer was not as used to the sometimes arduous work and the long hot days under the sun, but he was fairly strong too, and before long the work did not seem so hard, and the days not so long and hot. He was a good worker.

Quite often the work and odd jobs would lead Jer and I well back into the 450-acre farm I lived on, deep into the woods, to some secluded apple orchard walled in by the wild beech, pine, and hemlock. Had the rest of the population of the world somehow been abolished while we were out in the woods, removing a fallen tree from an old dirt road, or eradicating some basketball-sized white-faced wasp nest from an apple tree at our own enjoyed peril, we would have been not one bit the wiser until we ventured back for supper much later in the day. And if such a thing had really happened, back to those same woods I think I probably would have gone, possibly that very night, and perhaps I would have lived a full life, much better maybe than you might think.

There are so many bits and pieces, I don't know where to begin or how to make sense of them. The tractors, I guess. To be a farmer you must use tractors and be comfortable with them. I can think of many stories involving the tractors, like the time Jer jack-knifed one of the Massey Fergusons, coming down Old Baldy with a load of dirt, the time I let Jer travel on the front forks on top of four bins piled high, or the time he drove one of the Case 1210s over the bank.

One of my favourites was the time Jer and I were cutting back the woods along one of the orchards. I was driving the Case and we had a bin on the front forks with the chainsaw and limb-loppers in it. Jer was riding in the bin as well, and as I was driving along he laid down in it and tried to fall asleep. When Jer had gotten into the bin it was only a couple of feet off the ground. Seeing that Jer had his eyes closed, I slowly and stealthily began to raise the front-loader until it was as high as it could go as I drove along. I laughed to myself at this for some time, and I laughed even harder when I saw Jer's groggy head peek out from above the bin to bewilderedly peer around; he was now cruising along at about fifteen feet above the ground. Some people would have been a little angry, but Jer thought it was the best surprise ever. To wake up and look out expecting to be a couple of feet off the ground only to discover that he now had a most superior view.

Another good story is about the time I ran Jer over. It was inevitable really. Jer and I had set out on the diesel Massey Ferguson 135, a make common to almost every farm in the valley. It would probably be considered little, as far as tractors go, but with its sturdy build of solid steel, it's still considerably heavier than your standard car. Our job for the afternoon was to cut the tent caterpillar nests out of the apple trees. We enjoyed driving from orchard to orchard, eradicating the nasty infestation and tossing the nests into a bin we carried on the back forks. It was quite a light-hearted affair, and it began to have an effect on our souls and on the world and how we viewed it. We were puttering up the hill in Block 9 on the little Massey. I was driving, and Jer had decided to sit on the hood of the tractor, his legs dangling over the front of the grill. As we continued on we began to sing some song or another, something that we both knew all the words to—or at least the chorus, so we could belt that out at the top of our lungs, even if the verses might be slightly maundered. As we crept up the hill, the North Mountain loomed larger in front of us. I began to swing the steering wheel of the Massey back and forth to the rhythm of the song we were singing, so there was no way to avoid swaying in sync with the tune. How light the air, how free of inhibitions; you would never catch a couple of guys proceeding in such a fashion down the road of some busy city or town. But here, on the farm, with the North Mountain in the distance, the faint smell of seaweed enticingly blowing off the Atlantic, making a mind sensible of nautical thoughts, of perilous adventures, just with the absolute remoteness of it all, it seemed anything could go. We were free to act as we pleased, to assume the natural good-naturedness that people are endowed with at birth, only for it to be too often stifled and lost amongst the hectic lifestyles and fabricated dilemmas that people so often find themselves transferring their energy into. The strangling hassle of the everyday, the governing order, the adhering to, the constant race we all must run, the hoops we must jump; those old rules of life that we are constantly adding to, every generation making its own amendments, its own complications. The simplicity of life that philosophers pondered long ago, all but forgotten.... Right then, however, Jer and I, in the lee of the mountain, were living. We had found it again, that primal good naturedness, and we laughed at our fortune, although in a consumer's eyes we were very poor. Just when we both could not get any freer, and Jer was in danger of floating off the hood of the Massey and flying around, he fell off and I ran over him. What a crash that was, to be knocked down when we were both so high, so free, so caught up in it all, as they say. With one of the sways of the tractor, that were to the rhythm of some now forgotten song, Jer had slid off the hood, and I had run right over his ankle with my front tire. I had managed to stop before the large studded back tire reached him, but the song had stopped too. I watched as Jer rolled around on the ground. The only sounds I could hear now were the sparrows and finches twittering about the trees, the crickets in the grass, as though they were continuing on with their good time, but without us now. Hesitantly, unsure if I wanted to know, "Are you okay?" I asked.

Jer gave his ankle one last rub and to both of our great surprise, he stood up. "I think I most certainly am," he said.

The ground had been quite soft, and so the heavy tractor had merely pushed his ankle into the yielding grass and ground a bit, absorbing the heavy load in the same way that the woods sometimes absorb a heavy mind—and so it seemed the nature all around us really did want us to stay, and we thought we would. After all, we still had a couple more verses we wanted to sing.

Working was good, but an added perk to working on the farm were the salamander girls, as we called them. There were a few girls from the local university, Acadia, that were researching the salamanders on our farm. They were biology students. Due to our seclusion, and to the fact that there was a lack of viable women within a fairly large perimeter about our persons, these salamander girls seemed nothing short of goddesses who had been set free amongst us—goddesses who studied the yellow-spotted salamander, a favourite little creature of mine too, no less. The possibility of meeting up with one of the salamander girls made even the times they weren't around better.

The salamander girls had set up little screens with buckets on the ends of them for traps, and they would come around almost every day to check on them. Jer and I were going to be going to university in the fall. I will not have you think I am naive; the probability of a girl in her third or fourth year, or working on her master's, being interested in us was probably quite minimal, but still, they were always so nice, so beautiful, the sun on their hair, the black mud on their legs.... All was new, nothing about the salamander girls seemed possible, but we were young, and so it was nothing to have infinitely distant, impossible dreams.

It was an extremely warm morning, not even noon yet and already it was almost thirty degrees. We were 'up over the hill' as we called it, the phrase so familiar in my ears—almost like it is one word, for it describes a particular place—that it seems odd to have to explain it. So, up over the hill we were fixing bins. Along the side of the road on the way up, the grass and bushes were all covered in dust from the trucks and tractors going by. They needed a good rain to wash them off. We were on a little flattened section near the woods just off the corner of one of the fields, hundreds of bins piled five and six high just next to us. Twenty or thirty single bins were scattered about the yard, ones I had put there with the front-end loader. I would take quite a few bins down at a time and spread them out, so we did not have to listen to the loud diesel engine, which shattered the tranquility of the place, too often. The old grass around the fields stood bleaching in the sun. The spot we were on had almost no grass on it from the constant wear of the tractors stacking bins, but there was a little bit of short chamomile, with the little yellow ends on the stems. It smelled strongly when you walked over it, and it was easy to find a nail or something when you dropped one, better than the long grass. The crickets chirped in the shade, and under the stacked bins; the hawks shrieked as they cruised the skies, scouring the fields for mice. When you looked up to see them they were sometimes almost lost in the sun, faint silhouettes, circling. The grasshoppers clacked as they awkwardly flew along, bobbing and weaving. Occasionally a large one would land near you with a little tumble, only to quickly right itself. Finally, the true sign of a hot day, the soulful whine of cicadas would siren every once in a while, lasting for half a minute or more at a time, as they called out to each other in the heat. How I loved the sound of the cicada—such a gigantic insect, such a queer account to think that they would spend their first seventeen years in the ground, and now here one was, singing to the sun, as his kind had done for hundreds of years, no difference whether I was there or not.

The heat did not bother Jer and I—in fact we rather enjoyed it. We did not wear anything more than our sandals and our dusty old shorts as we hammered away, replacing broken boards and runners on the bins. We also quite enjoyed the fact that we each wore a carpenter's belt. Seemed to us like we had become quite the professionals. Once you got the belt filled with nails it would get pretty heavy, and it was almost impossible to avoid having a plumber's crack, even though neither Jer nor I had any fat on us to speak of. We thought it was pretty funny to be walking around with the belts with half of our asses hanging out. It seemed like the more ass was hanging out the funnier the whole thing was to us. I even thought that Jer and I should go on the road with this sort of comedy. Maybe we could do stand-up routines; the whole time, Jer and I would just walk around the stage without saying a word, shirtless, with our belts on and our asses hanging out, bending over to hammer on a board or something that had been placed on the stage as a prop, glancing over our shoulders every once in a while to check out the response of the audience. It went over pretty big up there on the farm anyways, up over the hill, I know that much.

As we worked we laughed at the belts and the half-asses and we would sing the song "And the sun was shinin …" but mostly just the chorus. Even though we usually could expect to see one of the salamander girls at least once in the day, we still didn't take too much care in making ourselves look too presentable for them. We were counting on our rugged good looks and carefree country-boy charms to do the work for us. My hair was fairly long, but short or at least stiff enough that when I woke up in the morning it usually stood straight on end. I was probably a good four inches taller when I woke up in the morning. On this particular morning I had even brushed my hair backwards, with my hand, so that all of my hair was standing on end. That, coupled with my belt and ass hanging out, made me a fairly witty guy as Jer and I saw it.

We were both hammering away when we saw the little blue Nissan sedan four-door, the vehicle of our favourite salamander girl, creep over the hill and slowly drive the dusty farm road towards us as though blown to us on some divine wind, a little cloud of dust hanging in its wake. We both pulled up our belts a little, but still let them hang a bit, wanting to show our humour. I stopped hammering and stood up to watch, the sun reflecting off my dark skin, the veins showing in my arms and hands from the heat and the labour, the muscles toned from constant use. I sucked a little more air into my lungs than usual as the car pulled up, puffing my chest out a little. I held the hammer loosely in one hand by my side. She stopped, and the dust picked up from her car continued on and passed her by a few feet before it again settled to the ground.

"Hi," she said.

"Hey."

"Hey," Jer said like a bullfrog.

"It looks like we're going to have another warm one," said the salamander girl, beaming that smile of hers.

"Yeah!" I said, with all the excitement of a little kid who's just been asked if he would like some ice cream, quite out of sync with the tone of the conversation heretofore. I felt as though I had to show some enthusiasm or something; I don't know why—to make her think I was a fun guy, I guess—plus she was smiling so happily herself, so that made me happy. I started to try and think of something to say, pausing and staring off into space for a second, thinking, something to prolong this conversation. I wished she'd called ahead, told us she would be stopping today to chat, so Jer and I could have been talking all morning about things that we could say. We often made little plans like that. We would talk about plans for hours. Sometimes three or four words from our mouths to a girl were the result of hours of careful planning and deliberation.

"I guess you're probably heading over to the pond at the bottom of Block 3 to check your salamander traps?" I said, squinting a little at my own dim-wittedness after I had said it, only desperate to be conversational, wondering how others did it, talking. She would not have even realized that the block above the pond in the direction she was heading was Block 3, and where the hell else would she be going? She probably had not come all this way to see Jer and I standing around with our asses hanging out, though it was very comical, as I have said. She also probably didn't come, I later thought, to sit there and listen to me state the obvious to her all day.

"Yep, I am off to check them," she said, still smiling, now almost laughing. "Well I don't want to keep you. You boys have a good day." We will now, I thought as she drove away, thinking it would not be bad to be kept for a bit, staring after her. The salamander girls. Me without a clue, but knowing there was something there I wished to know, or at least be closer to. Jer and I continued to stand and stare until her car disappeared along the little dirt road into the woods.

"Whoa, did you see the way she was lookin' at me and smiling?" I said as I turned to Jer.

"Yeah. You remember that you still have your hair all standing up don't you?"

"Oh yeah," I said reaching up and running my hand through my hair for a second, thinking.

"But still," Jer said, "she seemed unusually happy to see us this morning."

"Yeah, I know, that's what I was thinking," I said, getting into the act. "It's probably our rugged good looks, and our simple country-boy charms." I said with a straight face, as though serious. "Not so artificial like those university guys she is used to probably, what with their deviously smooth talk, their starched Tommy clothes and cologne … and their completely covered asses," I added. "Almost makes me sick to think about it," I was saying as I started to hammer in a nail again, still talking, still smiling.

"She probably doesn't really even have to check the traps today," Jer half jokingly speculated.

"Yeah ... probably not. She is a sly one, that salamander girl, but I'm onto her.... Hooo yeah, not much gets by the Haremeister these days ... no sir."

"Those women are not even going to know what hit them when they see us stroll onto campus this fall."

"Hmmph, it'll be somethin' anyway." I chuckled outright. "Really somethin'."

And now I get up to fetch myself another beer, but after a few hollers, instead of getting one I find I am getting four. The beer bottles in the fridge door rattle against each other as I open it. I begin to talk before I get back to my seat, raising my voice and talking from the kitchen.

I pass around the beer and I sit down again.... "We used to go pruning up in Block 13 sometimes," I begin, getting comfortable again in my seat. It was an orchard way back in the woods on the very side of the mountain, steep. The long road heading into it was like a tunnel, for the huge maples and poplars that towered and hung over it. I always enjoyed passing over the little spring-fed stream on the way into it; I would sometimes stop to get some water. Jer and I puttered up to the orchard on the tractor, hauling behind it the trailer with our pruning gear. The trailer was handmade, so to speak; it had a wooden deck and was fashioned from a large old truck axle. The trailer was infamous for having killed a guy once.

Well, now I know I have gone and made a mistake, for I won't be able to go on until I clean this up, and more fully explain myself. So here it goes.

About twenty years earlier the very same trailer was being used by a man and his son to haul wood. The wood was piled high and the son was sitting on top of it. As they travelled down a steep hill, not far from here, the stacked wood began to roll forward. The boy slid down right in between the tractor and the old trailer. The man tried to apply the breaks, but of course with such a steep hill and the heavy load, the man could slow but not outright stop and so he ran clean over the boy's head, and he soon found himself alone in those woods.... "And so think about that if you will," I say almost angrily, tensing up and on the verge of getting out of my seat, although not really angry at any of the people, maybe just a little angry, though only for a moment, at the very nature of the sometimes harsh life herself, and sad at the thought that she can't always spare.

I did not want to say it, but it had to be said, because it was what I remembered, and just like in life so in my story there are dark parts that must pass. And so I must pick up where I left off, and struggle back to my feet, to shake off the ill feelings, determined to lighten the mood once more, and to end it with that for the night. For the night, as it closes in on us, should be approached with a light heart and a chuckle, half drunk on one's own good emotions to endure any beasts that may lurk within.

I'm sorry. Where was I, oh yes ... so Jer and I were heading up to Block 13 to prune by ourselves, as I have said. We puttered along and took our time, but we did not drag our feet—we just took time enough to appreciate the drive, the trees, the stream, to live. The orchard had thousands of trees. Just the two of us could have pruned there forever, and after we'd reached the last tree so much time would have passed that we could have started at the beginning again had we wanted. The task was so big we could have wondered why we bothered, but we didn't. In the same way people have to carry on and not wonder too much about anything, for our plans in life at some point will inevitably be cut short, and so people must continue as though their life were an infinity at times, no matter at what point in their lives, always concentrating on what they can do, and never thinking or dwelling upon what will inevitably never get done. We talked of many things—of girls, of the prom, the disastrous prom—and we joked. The same jokes we told over and over and we laughed at them just like they were new. Maybe it was the sun, I don't know.

As we worked in the vigorously growing Delicious apple trees (that was the variety of the apples up there. I always thought it must have been intended as sarcasm. Give me a Gravenstein any day), we sometimes climbed up so as to better prune them. The handsaw was able to cut through a branch much faster than a pole saw. As we clambered over the smooth, light purple-coloured bark of the trees, we noticed there were a number of ants marching back and forth, sometimes in a line, going up and down the limbs and trunks. Jer and I, both appreciative of wildlife, even the diminutive ant, thought it was quite something to watch them going about their business, always in a hurry to get some bit of work done, not too unlike another certain species I know of. There were probably some aphids in the trees and the ants were tending to those. Ants are quite the farmers. They will tend and keep aphids like we keep cattle. They suck the nectar-like fluid off their backs; they carry them around in their pincers, sometimes into their burrows. They also culture fungus colonies down in their dens. Amazing really, the little ant. Anyway, I don't know who started it, Jer or I, or maybe we both chimed in at the same time, being so exactly of a mind and under the same conditions, out in the orchard. Out of nowhere, and to the tune of "O When the Saints Go Marching In" we started singing "O when the ants...." It was phenomenal, so spontaneous, so unprompted and from our hearts; we really wanted to sing. We just kept singing along, our voices never clashing. Sometimes there were little improv scats, sometimes we would sing in tune, sometimes I would sing high and Jer low, and sometimes Jer would do a little high part and I the low. It was all so good, to be a part of such a thing, I wished I had a tape recorder so we could somehow share this with the world. But we didn't have a recorder, and when the feeling passed we stopped. Amazed, we talked of what an excellent mantra it had been, the type of thing that you could learn something from, a memory for your pocket.

A few days later we tried to sing the ant song again, but it wasn't the same, and the song petered out before we reached the end, or even really had begun. We had gone into the thing with preconceived ideas, as though looking for the exact formula we had used. Jer and I were looking at each other trying to find the magic of that afternoon, but too earnestly, I'm afraid, and that just went against everything that the ant song stood for, and everything that was good about it. Like with the ant song, you can never go back, as they say—but you can always move forward. You have to in fact, where else can you go?

And now I see my beer is finished, and I don't think I need another. I can feel the silence coming; people continue to talk for a while. There are always many digressions and comments by others strewn throughout this type of evening—but they are growing shorter now, the silence is winning out, encompassing greater intervals, giving our minds the freedom to softly swim amongst the thoughts that have been prompted by the tales, the sacrosanct silence allowing us to privately explore, sun lower drawing gazes, voices tired, silence heavier ... there, I think that was it. The feeling's gone, or just changed, and like the others I guess I will allow the silence to creep over us again, just as the forest will creep over an old field that you no longer see fit to tend, and so take it over again, returning it to the most natural of states once more, as though nothing ever was; a cicada crawling up a tree after its long subterranean existence in the former clearing to give its soft soulful siren, unseen.

4 *Aerial Runway*

You never know what you might come across at a garage sale. There are always all sorts of odds and ends just waiting for the right person to come along to think of a use for them. There are lots of things that some people might walk right by without even thinking. We always had a keen eye for stuff like that. Sure, some of the things we purchased, we may not have had a clear idea of what we were going to do with them, and some of them may have sat around until someone who lacked our foresight complained about them, but sometimes the things we got from garage and yard sales really paid off. Here is the story of one of those times.

We were travelling down the Pereaux road coming back from Canning in one of the old Corollas. We might have been in the blue Corolla, the one that we called the blue Corolla even after it had been painted green. People still knew what you meant. Names are just names I guess. It would always be the blue

Corolla. Ron was driving and it was Scott, Matt and I in the back. Ron was the only one that had some sort of business in Canning; the rest of us never had business anywhere, for we were young enough that our business still travelled wherever we did, meaning it was always close at hand. We had just tagged along so we could run about Canning for half an hour or so, checking out the river and the small grocery store they had there. Stores were still a novelty for us, since they were things we did not see too often, living out in the back where we did.

So, not to make a short story long, we were travelling along the Pereaux road, headed home, when we spotted a sign advertising a garage sale. This guy always had a garage sale; he was one of those people that just left a sign out there and you could come in and rummage through his stuff. If you found something you wanted, you would have to go find where he was to see what the deal was; maybe he enjoyed the haggle, got something out of it. Usually people who use this kind of system have a whole heap of crap at their yard sales that you really don't want to look at. They usually have things like boxes of mismatched coffee mugs complete with coffee stains in them, letting you know they work all right, or cheap old lamps that may have been in vogue for a few years in the seventies, but now just appear chintzy. Most of these items I think people actually bought at other yard sales and then, after they got home, realized they were crap and would try to sell them again. They just couldn't stop themselves from buying things. Even though this guy always had a garage sale, though, his stuff was generally all right.

We had stopped at this guy's place a couple times before and we knew that every once in a while he had something that was pretty good. One time he had a couple of old guns, and another time he had an old motorcycle that didn't work. Even though we hadn't the money for the big-ticket purchases like these, we still liked to know about such deals being out there, just in case.

Seeing that we had no real plans set for when we got home, we decided we were in no hurry to get there. When we saw the sign for the garage sale, we all yelled for Ron to stop with such urgency that he probably thought that one of us had fallen out of the back or something again. I guess he was feeling a little carefree himself that day. He stopped the car and we all bolted out, running to the tables and darting from one object to another like a bunch of hummingbirds. Ron took his time, just seeming to enjoy the little walk and the fresh air as much as anything else. He also was probably pretty sure that the garage sale items were still going to be there by the time he got to them, so he didn't really need to rush.

The good thing about us was it didn't really take us long to scour a garage sale to see what there was to be had. As we were flying around, Ron would be casually looking at some object or another, which we had already flown over, or maybe the man that owned the stuff had come over to talk to him about the day. We had pretty well all finished our searching. We had all been over everything and had determined that there were no huge finds to be had that day. Our searching now more closely resembled Ron's. The first bit of excitement now gone, we all calmed down and just slowly picked up a thing here or there, really only half interested. As we were doing this I saw that Scott had a large roll of yellow nylon rope in his hand as he was looking at some other things in that half interested manner I spoke of. Matt and I, having finished our inspection completely at this point, walked over to him.

"You thinking you are going to buy that rope or something?" Matt asked, he and I looking at it, curious as to what Scott saw in it.

"Yeah," Scott said, he thought he would. The rope was kind of thin, so it really would not be that good for towing, but there was always a ton of things you could do with a rope, especially one that long. It was about 250 feet. The group of us walked over to the man who owned the place as though we were a pack of lawyers ready to negotiate the garbage pickup contract for the city of Halifax or something; we were all business. Scott did the talking since he was the one who was going to buy it. Matt and I just stood there looking at the guy like a couple of thin-yellow-nylon-rope experts ready to offer our services if a true appraisal was needed. The man said he'd take two fifty for it. This was fair; it seemed like a pretty good price for a rope that long. With a price like that most people wouldn't bother trying to go any lower.

"Fifty cents," Scott said. Matt and I sort of winced and turned away a little; the man just stared. Scott ended up buying the rope for two dollars.

On the way home in the car we all thought of things we could do with the rope. The first thing we all thought of was a swing. If we could find a suitable place to hang that sucker what a great swing it would make. But at the same time we all acknowledged that the rope was probably too thin for a swing. A rope so thin would cut into your hands, and besides, it was slick and would be hard to hold onto. When we got back we still hadn't thought of anything. We fixed ourselves a little snack and just sort of sat around for a while, pretty much giving up on the ideas for a long nylon rope, at least for a while. Later that day Scott and I were rummaging around some junk in the barn, probably onto some new thing, when we came across a pulley. Suddenly our thoughts sprung back to the yellow rope still coiled and sitting on the table in the kitchen—coiled in the most unassuming manner, oblivious to all the glories that it was to behold in due course.

We attached the pulley high up in one of the maple trees and used the rope to hoist things up. You know, just the usual things one would need to hoist way up into a tree: old logs sitting around, a rock, things of that nature. Now, it seems the natural notion of a boy when he sees this set-up is to try and hoist himself into the tree. The problem was, as soon as you got off the ground you had no balance and you would start to fall backwards. Your natural reaction seemed to be to raise the top half of your body by pulling harder on the rope. The only thing was, the harder you pulled on the rope the faster your feet got whipped into the air, leaving you to do a backflip and literally land on your head. This happened to both Scott and I. We both thought it was quite something how we didn't even think about that and how your natural instincts could get you into so much trouble. When Paul and Matt came by later we thought it fit not to tell them until after they had tried it. Things like that were better figured out by yourself—plus it was more humorous that way.

A day or so had passed, and most things that needed hoisting into trees had already been hoisted. Scott and I were out in the yard; I was half contemplating trying to hoist myself up into the tree, but then we had a better idea. This was unparalleled brilliance. Scott and I had the idea that we could tie the one end of the long rope high up in one of the oldest, biggest maples around, near the house. The other end we would tie up in a smaller tree on the other side of the gully. After the idea dawned on us we could think of no better thing to do with such a long piece of rope. It was relatively simple to set up. We tied the one end of the rope about twenty feet up in the old maple; then we attached the big round pulley. We ran the rope across the gully and tied it up on the other side, using the come-along, a manual lever and winch system, to get the rope as singing tight as possible. Setting it up was the easy part; the next thing we had to do was use it.

By the time we had gotten it all set up, Matt and Paul had come around to see what this aerial runway business was about. We brought out the extension ladder and put it against the maple; this was to be the launching ladder, where people could catch the express route across the gully. We were revolutionizing the way gullies were to be crossed in Pereaux forever. Like fools we used to hoof it across that gully on our own two feet. The trek *used* to take several minutes, climbing down the hill, weaving around bushes, and then climbing up the other side. Now we would be able to cross the gully in mere seconds. Our great-grandchildren would probably think about us when they crossed gullies on their aerial runways in the future; by that time the pulley would probably be rocket powered or something. Anyway, the point is we were really doing something, and really doing something that you could talk about, and people wouldn't mind listening.

The only problem with the aerial runway in the beginning was that it was a little intimidating, and no one was really sure if they wanted to go on it. Even the launching point off the ladder in the tree was pretty high off the ground, and it was on the side of the steep gully. The land just kept dropping out from under you from there. In the middle of the gully the rope was forty feet off the ground, not the sort of height any of us were keen to fall from. We were a pretty rough-and-tumble bunch, but even we had our limits. The other thing was you had to trust Scott's and my knot-tying ability. None of us had ever gone to Boy Scouts or anything like that, so we weren't experts in the field, but we all were of the opinion that nothing could beat the old granny knot.

There was a pro and a con to being the first one to go on the aerial runway. The con was there was a chance you could fall and seriously damage yourself. The pro was you would be known, at least amongst Scott, Matt, Paul and myself, as the guy who was the first one to go on the aerial runway, and it would go down in the annals of adventure. We all were just standing around there at the base of the ladder waiting to see if there would be any volunteers from the crowd. Finally Paul, as though he had just got the crazy feeling, said he would do it and he quickly began to scale the ladder, climbing pretty fast in case the feeling was a fleeting one. The problem was that it was a long old climb up to the top of the ladder. Scott had climbed up the tree itself and was on a big branch next to the ladder, handing Paul the short piece of rope that we had hanging down from the pulley. We had put a bar on the end of it so it looked sort of like a trapeze. By the time Paul took the rope from Scott and turned around it was too late; the feeling was gone. Paul would have to wait to try and find it again. He stood there looking out over the gully with the rope in his hand for some time. The rest of us stood around staring at him. Sometimes we would be loud, yelling taunts up at him and trying to give him some courage; at other times we were all very quiet, letting Paul gather his thoughts to prepare for the big plunge. This cycle of taunts and then silence was repeated a few times. Finally we got tired of waiting; it did not look like Paul was going to go. No one really blamed him. Everyone was scared of it and wanted to see someone else try it to make sure it would hold up before they were willing to give it a try. Secretly, on the ground, I had been preparing myself for jumping off the ladder and letting the aerial runway take me away. I imagined it not being so bad. Finally I told everybody I was sure I would do it, and Paul climbed down to let me give it a go.

Paul's big mistake was waiting for so long; after that initial hesitation, the odds of him going for it steadily and steeply went down, in direct relation to how long he waited. Once you were up there your mind did everything it could to try and talk you out of it, and if you listened for long enough, it started making sense. I resolved to hardly wait at all. Once up there Scott handed me the bar and I saw what Paul had been staring at. It was by this time a little after supper. It had been a warm summer day, but it was now a little darker than it had been. The sun was getting lower. Soon there would be a beautiful sunset off in the west. I stared out over the gully. I heard the crickets chirping down in the long grass. The taut rope was humming because of a slight breeze that was blowing across the gully. I looked up at the North Mountain ahead of me. It seemed so majestic, covered with its pine, beech and poplar, off in the distance. I was still a lot lower than the mountain, I reasoned in my head, the logic apparently quelling any doubts I might have had. By the time I had taken all this in I realized I was starting to stall. My mind was dividing. It was beginning to build the logic for me not to go at all, the innocent part of my mind almost unaware but listening. You have to clear your head of all things, of all thoughts, free your mind, become as light as the air. I looked up at the leaves, and then down at the rest of the guys on the ground. Scott was a little behind me in the tree and I knew he was grinning with anticipation. Scott was one of the engineers of the whole project, waiting to see if his design could take the hurricane.

I was pretty well ready to go and then I looked at

 a maple leaf next to my head; there was a little ant crawling around on it. I wondered what it was up to. It probably never really even considered flying out of this tree … or maybe it had. I decided I would do this ant a little favour, give it something to tell the other ants back at the hill, give it the thrill of its ant lifetime. I put my finger next to the ant and it crawled on. Then I touched my finger to my arm and the ant crawled off onto my shirt, still searching, no different than it had been on the leaf. With that done, I grabbed the bar with both hands and jumped out. I wasn't just doing this for me anymore. I was doing it for the guys on the ground, Scott grinning in the tree, and the ant crawling around on my shirt. I'd be selfish not to go, people were counting on me. I quickly dropped about five feet, my weight taking up what little slack there was in the rope. I accelerated quickly and I shot down into the gully, the wind blowing through my hair. This was the closest to flying I had ever been. I continued to pick up speed as I approached the centre of the gully. I actually dropped a fair bit as the rope bowed. At the centre I was only about twenty feet off the ground. A lot of things were blocked out as I flew through the air. I didn't hear anyone yelling, the crickets chirping, or even take notice of the mountain or the trees on it. I heard the whizzing sound of the pulley on the thin little rope, the sound rising in frequency with the increased speed, and I saw the rope stretching out in front of me. I bobbed when I reached the lowest part of the run, the middle of the gully. My momentum started carrying me up the other side, my feet still dangling high above the grass and bushes, now decelerating, but still moving pretty fast. My mind had spent so much time preparing itself for the start of this journey that I had never given the stopping part much thought. It soon sorted itself out, though, in the form of me crashing into a bunch of bushes relatively safely. The smell of the broken bayberry bush filled my nose. I heard a cheer rise up from the crowd back at the maple tree. I let go of the bar and it sprung into the air as if shot from a bow, only to hit the top and come flying back at me, but with some scrambling on my part it missed, and it didn't take away from anything, maybe added to it.

This was a big day for me; this was a big day for all of us. I noticed the ant was still crawling around on my shirt. I wondered if it had even noticed the ride I had just taken it on. I felt as though I should give some sort of speech or something, something that would fill the rest of the guys with pride, something that would fill them with the feeling that we were all driving forward and as long as we kept thinking of things like the aerial runway, forward towards greatness we were destined to always go. Something like the famous words of Neil Armstrong when he landed on the moon. I couldn't think of anything though, the words just weren't there. There'd only be one first trip on the aerial runway, with the fear, the ant by my side. My head was still filled with that euphoric feeling from flying across the gully. I didn't need words; words would have been nothing. I felt silly and small just standing there trying to put what I felt into words. Who'd I think I was anyways? Everybody knew what the aerial runway was and what we had done. When the guys came over I just told them they should give it a try, which of course everyone did, time and time again.

We made some adjustments. When you fell off at the other end, the bar was left twenty feet in the air, so we had to attach another long piece of thinner rope onto the bar, which allowed you to drag it back to the maple once you had reached the other side. We also looked into ways to make the rope tighter. A system was set up using the old white Corolla hatchback. Other than that, the aerial runway was all we had hoped for and more. We had really done something. This was something you could talk about and people would take notice. I wondered what other people did with their time—crawling around like ants for the most part I thought. How close I felt to the world that day, and how far away from it all; the proud North Mountain in the distance, crickets still chirping like they always had in the tall grass.

5 *The Basement*

We always thought of the MacInnises' basement as a dark, foreboding spot. Along with the natural darkness, the basement seemed to harbour some unnatural darkness—or maybe just a forgotten depth of natural darkness, which had leaked in from somewhere, and settled. It was similar to that feeling you get when you hear the coyotes strike up a howling chorus up in the woods, in the hills of the valley. Their voices seem to invite something, it seems like other things join—nothing definite, nothing prominent, but a faint urgent reminder, the voices ringing against each other and travelling through the forests, unroosting and shaking past spirits from the land and trees with their vibrations like the dampness from a bough. This quality of present and past meeting was in the basement. Basement is probably the wrong word here; I guess it would be better to refer to it as a cellar. It was large, so as to suit the house. The floor was, for the most part, sand, with a few cement aprons that had been put in many years ago. The walls were large stones, stones that someone had plucked out of the field and fashioned over a hundred and fifty years before. They were the same stones you saw just lying around outside. They were the same stones that some of the poorer people in the area used to fashion their gravestones with. The old Pereaux Cemetery—our quietest neighbours on that dead-end dirt road—was a testament to that. It was always damp down there, damp and cool. A little bit of moss managed to grow on the stone walls. The basement was cut up quite a bit. There were walls jutting out here and there and it seemed like a catacomb. One little room looked like it was created to be a root cellar. It was small, and there were a bunch of shelves in there. There were a couple of ancient, broken Mason jars sitting on the shelf, and also a couple of intact ones whose contents were now mysteries. There were two cells made out of brick against one of the basement walls. They were both the same size, about six by six. The walls came up from the floor, but they stopped at about six and a half feet, leaving a gap of a couple feet between the top of the walls and the ceiling. They may have been there originally to hold some sort of a boiler or something, but to us it seemed more likely they were built to cage in something sinister long ago. When you looked inside them there was just a bunch of garbage now. You could not actually see anything sinister, but that did not mean anything. It only meant that the sinister thing was no longer being held, but was free.

The door to the basement was in the kitchen/living-room area. When you opened the door you went down a short passageway on some steep creaky stairs; each step was short, shorter than your foot. The stairs went straight down, with a wall on your left and the open basement on your right, until you hit the wall of the foundation, then there was a landing and the stairs took a right turn and continued down until you were at the bottom. At the top of the stairs, the part that was still sort of in the first storey of the house, the walls were crumbling plaster, which had been papered over with newspapers from the forties and fifties. These were actually sort of interesting to stop and read, if you were in a lighter mood. When you got below the first storey of the house the walls turned back into the fieldstone I mentioned. At the landing, there were a couple of little wooden doors tucked in amongst the stones, with old-fashioned handles on them. There was one each on the north and west walls. They were about a foot-and-a-half by a foot-and-a-half in size. The wood was not painted, but it had turned grey with age. The grain of the wood had become exposed as happens with old wood; you could feel the ridges of the years with your fingers. These two little doors opened into some relatively wide, but only three-foot high, crawl spaces. I'm not sure what they were used for. Maybe they were another place to keep things cold at one time. There was a lot of sand in them. The floor was all sand; you could dig straight through to the other side of the earth if you wanted to. I remember one time we found some bones in one of these crawl spaces, which we never could identify.

We would always hang out in the kitchen. It was the warmest part of the house. There was a wood stove in the corner that was usually burning hot. There was a couch, and a couple of chairs that we would always sit in. The chairs were big, comfortable armchairs. They were as heavy as anything. Ron had gotten them at the huge old wooden train station that used to be in Kentville. It had been built out of wood in the days when the trains were a booming business. The tracks used to come right on out to Apple Tree Landing (now unfortunately renamed Canning). Canning, quite a majestic place in its heyday, used to be known for its wooden shipbuilding business, before the aboiteau was put in; ships of around four hundred tons, like the *Bahama* that went down off Cuba, or the *A. B. Barteaux*, or the *Blomidon* that was launched into the then tidal Habitant River in 1919. They used to say that on the launch day the people would swell into the dockyards with the tide, the crowd slowly growing. It would be a big day, and people would say as they walked around, "You going down?" Rolly Porter, who used to live in the MacInnises' house, remembers those days when wooden three-masters would be launched in the Habitant. There's no time to talk about Rolly now though, you'll meet him later.

The railway continued through Canning and on to Kingsport, where the tracks went right out onto a huge wooden pier which extended into the expansive Minas Basin. There the train would deliver the Valley's apples, and other produce, in barrels off onto ships. The ships would take the apples to London and New York and all over the world. Those tracks were gone now. Where they had travelled through the woods only dirt bikes went now. There used to be tracks going everywhere, when things were bustling, but most of those were gone, too. There was still the one main track that went through Kentville, but the train hardly ever ran. The station no longer needed to be anywhere near the size it was, and the money was no longer there for something that size either. It didn't need to be a twentieth that size. They were only using one room of it, at that point. The rest was just storage. They auctioned off some of the old stuff in there before they tore it down. I think Ron may have even gotten the chairs for free. I believe they were from a passenger car. They had no feet on them, and parts of them were stuffed with hay. It looked as though they were once secured to the floor somehow. Even that hay must have been some old. I wonder how long ago it had been since that hay had been growing in a field somewhere, just blowing in the wind, bleaching in the hot sun. The chairs were so big they must have been in the upper-class car, the one that the wealthy businessmen and the rich would have travelled in. Maybe they travelled across Canada, from the Atlantic to the Pacific many times over. I wonder if anyone of special interest had sat in those chairs as they travelled across the country. Now the chairs had found their new home in the kitchen next to the stove, not too far away from the basement door.

One of the things that really made us wary of the basement was the handle on the door. It was an old latch. It had a handle that you would wrap your fingers around. Above that there was a round dimpled piece of steel that you would push down on with your thumb. When you pushed down on the lever it lifted up on the bar on the other side, releasing it from a catch so that you could open the door. The lever on the door was pretty loose and would sometimes act up. The same scene played itself out a number of times. We would all be sitting around the stove on the two train seats and the couch, lazily talking about something or other, when we would hear a rattling noise. We would look over, and always, to our amazement, we would see the latch rattling and clacking. There was no explaining it. We dismissed the idea of a draft just by the nature of the movement and the noise. A draft could not do this. It would start up suddenly and then cease just as suddenly. The conversation, of course, would be dead. All of our eyes would be locked on the latch. "Clack, Clack … Clack, Clack, Clack … Clack, Clack." The movement was so sudden and so calculated, it was as though some unseen thumb was slamming down on the lever, not even making an effort to be silent, to quietly slip into the room. It would usually only rattle like this for twenty seconds or so. A couple times the rattling was so violent that the lever actually fell out of the door and clattered to the floor. One time Paul, very timidly, but at the same time displaying much bravery, opened the door while this was going on. Scott, Matt and I were all on our absolute guard and ready for just about anything. But what was behind the door was dreadful … there was absolutely nothing, just pitch blackness. Not even a breath of air, just nothing. Somehow this seemed worse than something, nothing.

When the rattling had stopped, our voices would always drop down low and quiet. We would eventually settle back into the chairs, the couch, and we would talk; about the darkness in the world, and about other things these happenings would bring to mind.

So the basement was known as a dark place, where dark things happened. I remember one time when the rest of us were off elsewhere in the expansive farmhouse, Paul went down into the basement by himself to get something. He was not down there long when he came back yelling bloody murder. What he reported both shocked and amazed us, and only reinforced our thoughts about the basement. The lights had been out so he had used a flashlight, just a small one with a thin beam. The basement lights were not very good even when there was power. There were only a couple of bulbs rigged up from the ceiling. He was walking just beside where the two cells were and just in front of the little room that had once been a root cellar. Suddenly, out of the darkness that surrounded his beam of light, there was a shrieking sound. Darkness tends to weigh things down; your hearing becomes all the more acute to try and pick up even the most minuscule sounds that now seem to be more important, intensifying the silence. The screaming continued in the darkness, piercing this heavy silence. Paul's heart raced; he madly shone the light around, the thin beam only ever landing on an entirely too-small area. Finally his light found the frenzied creature. It was one of the giant rabbits that lived around there. It was pure white. We all knew the rabbits occasionally crawled in through a little hole in the north side, so they could come in out of the elements for a little while. There was something crouched over the giant rabbit, tearing into it while it was still alive. The creature had a long, seemingly too long, back that arched as it bent over. Its head was small compared to its body, but full of sharp canine-like teeth. In a flash the thing turned around, the blood still dripping from its jowl, to stare into the light, its eyes greenly reflecting the beam. Then it disappeared, leaving the bunny dead, but still kicking in its throes. Only an instant after the thing had disappeared Paul heard it right next to his head. He flashed around to see the creature only a few feet away, looking at him from atop one of the cell walls. Paul dropped the flashlight and took off full speed up the stairs, closing the door behind him. And that's when we met him and he told us what he had seen. This was hard to do, since he was not sure what he had seen.

At first Matt, Scott and I mocked Paul for being afraid of "the thing in the basement," maybe to cover our own fears. We weren't sure if he was telling the truth, or if in fact he was trying to trick us. We knew that if he was telling the truth our mocking would mean very little to him, in the same way his mocking would have meant little to us. We knew that if we had been him, we would have been no less afraid. We all had active imaginations, and a healthy awareness. Paul knew this. You never take mockings seriously from someone you know is no different than yourself.

When we saw that Paul was in earnest, we secured ourselves some larger flashlights and followed him back down to the scene. All of us were mentally preparing ourselves for the very worst of evils. Paul's flashlight was still on the ground, misguidedly shining its little beam of light on the rock wall and showing us absolutely nothing, but blinding our eyes to other things that may have been waiting in the darkness. We could not find the devil anywhere. Some of us were beginning to wonder about Paul's story, but then he showed us where the rabbit lay. There it was, dead all right. The fact that it was white seemed to make the scene grizzlier. You could see where something had torn into its neck. The blood looked very familiar, it looked just like my blood. That somehow made it all seem worse, to see my blood on the now dead rabbit.

After finishing a complete survey, we took care of the rabbit. We spent the next couple of hours talking about the scene, and of what we could possibly do about it, if anything. The rest of us had not seen any further signs of the creature; we weren't sure what it could have been. Later, when Ron got home, he suggested that it might have been a mink, a fisher, or a weasel or something of that sort. We decided to conduct a little research, which entailed breezing through the MacInnises' trusty old *Encyclopaedia Britannica*. The encyclopaedias were old, maybe thirty years, but really, as we figured, what had changed in that time? Not too much at the end of a dead-end dirt road. We found some pictures of minks and things. Paul thought it might have been a mink, but he couldn't be sure. The one in the picture was in a tree, just sitting there peacefully, not crouched over a screaming rabbit.

None of us were sure what it could have been. In the days that followed we found out that the creature was not yet finished. Each day we found more and more things that it had left behind. One day it was a couple of rabbits, the next we found a chicken. The day after that two chickens went missing. This was becoming epic. None of us really ever did get a good look at the elusive predator, but we kept finding what it left behind. Who was next, we began to wonder? This seemed like a lot of death for a mink or whatever it was. What if it was something more? What if it was some dark supernatural force that was only starting out with the small animals, leaving them about, as a warning of the power it wielded. It started seeming more and more logical. Things we knew and things that had seemed sure no longer seemed so sure. The world started to take on a dark undertone. We were starting to have that dark, mysterious, wondering feeling that we got after seeing the latch rattle. We did not even have to see the latch rattle, we did not even have to see the latch, the feeling was all over. The darkness that had once been generally restricted to the basement was now spreading. It was dark, but at the same time strangely exhilarating. People are fascinated by the darkness, the darkness and the unknown. But the creatures around the yard, were dying. This thing, whatever it was, had to be stopped.

Finally, one day, while we were all away somewhere, Ron saw the thing out on the outside basement doors. They were the large storm cellar doors you often see on old farmhouses, double doors on a slight angle, but almost flat, butted up against the house. When you opened them there were steep cement steps leading down into the basement. Ron grabbed the single-shot .22. He levelled the gun with a steadiness that is only acquired with the calmness of age. We boys would have been too fidgety to do such a thing. Being young, we'd have tried to look at too many things at once, to think about too many things at once. But Ron knew what the task at hand was, and he knew a lot of other things we didn't know. He fired the gun and the shot struck the creature straight between the eyes and it dropped. It was a mink. The eradicator of rabbits, and the black scourge of the chickens, was a mink. Its end was brought with the simple shot of a .22, which dropped it soundlessly to the ground in a lifeless mortal heap. Later Ron sold the pelt to another man for ten bucks.

After that we no longer found so many dead critters about the property. The killings were explained and the evidence presented. You might think that the dark and haunting thoughts we all had developed would have been eradicated like the mink had been. And they were a little bit, but not completely. The darkness retreated, back into places like the basement where it had always hid and lived. In our spirits we could sense that, but none of us were foolish enough to think it was completely gone. The handle still rattled and fell out every now and again. We knew the darkness would always be there, waiting for its next chance to seep out.

Later I learned not to have anything against the mink. It was only looking out for itself. I felt bad that it had to die. The mink was not dark, but there were things that were. Darker things not suited for a story about a little mink. We were part of the same vicious cycle that it was. Maybe that is the scariest part. I saw a few other minks after that, years later. There was one that always hung out by the creek. It would look at me, and I would look at it and wonder how the fishing was going, and if it was somehow related to a certain other little mink.

6 *Barebone, Moonlit Wonders*

There were lots of pastures around our place when we were young. I can remember a sunny day, just after suppertime, when I was four years old. We had a tent set up in the front yard. I had gone out there with my older brother and sister, Rob and Heidi. Now they had left and I was sitting there in the tent playing around—just enjoying the fact that I was camped out inside of a tent. In the distance I thought I could hear something. At first I couldn't be sure; it was a gradual crescendo—the earth seemed to rumble. Apparently the great creatures that rumbled about in the pasture down the road, usually safely behind the sharp wires, had broken through again. They came at a good pace down the road, and then they crossed the ditch so as to graze on the bright green grass that was our front lawn. There were probably around fifty or sixty of them. There were full-grown ones and adolescent ones, one massive male, some younger ones, and a couple little ones that bawled, just following wherever their mothers went. I was still inside the tent when they crossed onto the lawn. The sun was setting, and it shone crosswise directly onto the tent. The next thing I knew, the sun was casting giant shadows onto the walls around me. The tent acted like a screen for me on the inside, all those large silhouettes. Sometimes when they got close, the creatures' shadows would cover the whole tent; when they passed there would be brightness again. They had surrounded me. My first conclusion was that they were dinosaurs. They were massive. I did not know what to think. They were loud as well, the snorts and snuffling sounds they made so guttural. It was the deep sort of sound that only an animal of that size is capable of making, emanating from the deepest-most part of its diaphragm. The world seemed a wild place.

So I developed a healthy awareness of these lumbering creatures when I was still quite young. I passed this on to the others, but maybe they already knew; of course they did. There were pastures set up all around in the country out where we were. The old rusty barbed wire fences ran through the woods and thick mires and over the hills. The posts were grey and spotted with lichen. Sometimes there weren't even any posts; the brown wire would just be attached to a tree or something. Sometimes it passed right through a large old pine or any of the old trees; there were a lot of pines though. Over the years the tree would grow around the wire and they would become one. Quite often when you were way out in the middle of the woods somewhere you would come upon a fence running along. Sometimes you could only wonder if you were on the inside of the fence or on the outside. You didn't really want to be on the inside—at least, not if you thought you might not be alone. I don't think any of us owned an article of clothing that did not have a hole pulled out of it from where we had caught it on a piece of barbed wire. Even when you were careful, it was hard to avoid getting caught by the stuff. As the wire aged and rusted, the points thinned and grew sharper; it seemed as though it got deadlier with age.

A lot of the woods around there acted as pasture sometimes. The fences were arranged in such a way that different sections of land could be cordoned off at different times. You could never be too sure which pasture the animals were in. We would scout out a pasture and deem it pretty safe. Usually we would only cross a pasture when it was a necessary shortcut to where we were going. Occasionally we would find ourselves in the middle of crossing a supposedly empty pasture only to see a whole herd come rolling out of the woods. You had to worry about the large males the most. Sometimes they could be quite ornery and would chase us. The large male could always tell if you were nervous—or maybe he could sense a guilty conscience.

It was hilly around there. To get from meadow to meadow the herds sometimes had to cross over some rough terrain. It wasn't uncommon for one of the cattle, while trying to go down a steep hill or drumlin, to lose its footing, fall to the bottom, and occasionally break its neck. It would break its neck if it was lucky, break its leg if it wasn't. On the other hand, I guess if it was lucky it wouldn't break anything at all, or even fall in the first place, but there you go. I guess that would be a better definition of lucky.

Right at the bottom of the MacInnises' driveway there was a nice green piece of pasture. It was often full. Bordering it along the one side there was a creek, and on the other side of the creek there was a thick forest that went up a steep hill. I can't remember who noticed it first, but soon we all knew about it. One day Paul, Scott, Matt and myself were walking along the fence. We had just turned the corner and were heading into the sandy part of the road at the bottom of the driveway. It was a sunny day; every once in a while a cicada would sing out. You knew it was a warm day when you heard the cicadas. The crickets, unlike the cicadas, were always chirping—never when you got right next to them but always just a little ahead of and behind you by the road. Chirping and hiding under a broad leaf, or a piece of wood. Just as we got to the part where the road turned into the sandy bottom of the MacInnises' driveway at the foot of the hill, someone noticed that in the pasture, about two hundred feet away, at the base of the hill right next to the woods, there was something gleaming white. It was in there quite a ways. The sun reflected off the whiteness and you could definitely tell that something unusual was there. After that, when we would walk by in the middle of the night, when there was a full moon, we would see it in the moonlight; you could see it best by the moon, when white things glow. The full moon, the tides, stories from the mental institution; I've heard nurses say that at the hospital there is a spike in births every full moon. They say it with their eyebrows raised a little, like they're happy there is something they don't understand. At night we knew for sure there was something to the whiteness at the bottom of the hill. We thought it might be the remains of one of those lumbering creatures, something we could get close to if we dared.... We weren't sure. I couldn't quite make it out.

It was in a most dangerous spot. Right there on the border of the open field and the shielding woods. Even if you didn't see any cows in the open pasture you couldn't be sure if there were any in the woods. A whole herd would come down the hill at the same time; once they got up steam they couldn't stop themselves, either. They would just keep building speed. I don't know how many times we'd seen a whole herd just come bursting out of those woods on the hill. At first you would scarcely even hear them, only a faint rumbling sound so soft that you couldn't quite be sure what it was you were hearing—just like when I was four. Then the rumbling and the groans and bellows would intensify. You could tell they were near, but you wouldn't exactly know where in the woods they were. Suddenly, with a crashing and snapping of sticks and branches, they would break from the woods, come crashing down into the creek, only to climb up the bank on the other side and spill out onto the open green pasture. They would cross that creek like nothing. The cattle were a lot more agile than most would think. A few of them would mosey down to the creek to get a drink, and graze on the fresh green grass that lined its banks. Some would splash along the sandy bottom, scaring trout, their backs level with the banks on either side. The creek over the centuries had carved the ground away. When the herd had crossed the creek they would no longer stay in the compact group they assumed when they were really moving somewhere. They'd wander away and distance themselves from each other, give themselves room to graze, like it was time to relax.

In my case, we knew that if those cows were coming from the woods, and if, in mid-descent, they saw a couple of inquisitive boys down there at the base of the hill, trying to figure out what it was that shone so white, they wouldn't be able to stop. Maybe they wouldn't want to stop. The mystery of what the white thing in the pasture was continued for some time. The cows were always there, and if they weren't, we were sure they must be hiding right there in the woods where we couldn't see them. Just waiting for one of us to wander in there so they could come crashing down. We figured there was more going on in the head of a creature like that than meets the eye.

One time Scott and I decided to venture into the pasture. There were a lot of cows in the open field, but they were all on the other side. There was still a chance there would be some in the woods, but Scott and I figured that with so many animals in the open field the chances weren't as great. As soon as we started going over the fence all the creatures turned around and stared at us. They always stare. They would just stand there, almost frozen, staring and chewing their cud. Scott and I slowly started walking towards the whiteness, towards the answer to the nagging curiosity in our heads. Roughly ahead of us and off to one side stood the animals. Obviously we were seen, but we figured if we moved slow enough, acted as casual as we could, maybe they wouldn't start. It was a tricky business, this assumed nervous casualness. The ground was compacted a fair bit by the great weight of the creatures, and they kept the grass short, although it was still a brilliant green. It got its fair share of fertilizing. It was easy to walk over. The only things the animals hadn't eaten were a few small patches of goldenrod here and there, and the occasional lone Canadian thistle, the grass chewed to within a couple inches of the ground all around its base. Those thistles would grow out there even in the hottest summer. Their beautiful purple flowers never wilted a bit; their vicious spikes warding everything away, their hardness keeping the water in. With numerous sets of eyes scattered about the pasture following our every move, we really didn't want to make any false steps. We would first look down at the ground for a second, to get an idea of where all the patties and thistles lay in front of us, then after we got an idea where they were we would look back up and take a few careful steps, only to look down at the ground once again. We covered about a hundred feet or so in this fashion.

Suddenly, on the other side of the field, the great patriarch made an aggressive move; he wasn't fooled. He was huge, black with large horns, his chest almost the size of the MacInnises' Tercel. We froze, our hands out on either side of us so we could easily move either way. The beast froze too; it was intently staring at us now to see what our next move would be. Scott and I both, conceiving the same idea at the same time, sprinted towards the base of the steep grade, near the creek, where the mysterious whiteness was. The Tercel-chested animal started too, towards the same destination. We each got about fifty feet further, and then, seeing where our pursuer was, Scott and I—with one final glance at the white thing—wheeled and ran back towards the fence, faster and with more conviction than before. We could hear the animal snorting and pounding the earth with its hooves. This time we did not climb over the fence, but slid under it in a predetermined spot where we knew the bottom wire wasn't too close to the ground. Our hearts pounding, breathing heavily, we skidded under the fence with little time to spare. Not quite trusting the rusty barbs, we sprinted a little further and turned around. The animal had stopped, about fifteen feet from the fence. It was still madly staring at us; its breath was laboured like ours. We stood there for a moment thinking about what had happened, and then I saw a couple of the heifers out back break their frozen positions to bend down and resume their chewing. They continued on, life as usual. A few more of the cows eased up and continued about their business; they probably knew something, maybe thought the bull a little much sometimes, maybe joked about it amongst themselves. The bull still stared, but something eased at that point inside Scott and I as well.

We continued on up the driveway towards the house. Just as we entered the woodsy part of the driveway on the outside of the fence, I turned around to see where the bull was. It was sauntering on back to its herd. I think he had had fun. Now the whole herd was back to chewing up the grass. A few cows looked up, still chewing on their cud, to watch the bull coming back to them, greeting him with their eyes.

"Did you see anything?" Scott said.

"Yeah, I think it's a skeleton. I think I made out the skull, and a few ribs."

"Yeah, that's what I thought I saw too. Must have tripped coming down the hill."

"That's what I figure.... That's pretty crazy isn't it?" I said softly, shaking my head.

"Yeah," Scott said, and that was all he said.

7 *Fateful Zucchini*

We were deep into late summer, and the days didn't get much lazier. The dust would kick up from the sandy driveway as you walked over it, the grass turned a duller shade, and the green of the old maples and the huge willow that was situated out front like a garrison was saved only by their long roots, which stretched deep into the ground to unknown depths. It was late in the day, maybe around seven or eight, and we were enjoying the last of the light the summer evening had to offer. We had just returned home from town with a couple of bags filled with food we had bought. We were the only ones home, but that was familiar.

In the kitchen, the life centre of the house, there were a couple of massive Zucchini sitting in an ornate wicker basket. They were situated in such a manner that you knew their placement was the result of some careful artistic consideration. They were probably ten or fifteen pounds each, a monument to their kind, a testament to the fertile soil the house was surrounded by, a topic of conversation at a dinner party over a few drinks. I had caught a glimpse of this before, standing to the side, looking on. I'm not sure if I know what I saw. As someone sipped on a Caesar or a strawberry daiquiri, those Zucchini would practically speak for you. With a few drinks, the Zucchini, and the heat of summer, you would almost marvel at your own words like a third person, how easily they flowed. Soon the talk would evolve to the point that you would no longer be talking of Zucchini at all, but of far loftier topics of conversation. Those Zucchini weren't meant for boys, oh no. Maybe we did not see them for what they were, or maybe, still being boys, we found all too much that still deserved our marvelling, and so it was impossible to greatly discern one marvel from another, there only being so much credit and greater deference you can spread around.

If there was one thing in that house that was to be intact when Ron got home, it was those Zucchini. It was one of those things that seemed small and simple, but Ron had taken an interest in those Zucchini as of late. Forget about the way the door on the Corolla no longer shut as well as it should, don't ask about the scorch marks on the porch, never mind that there appeared to be a large hole dug out in the lawn, but for Christ's sake, and for the love of God, do not touch those Zucchini that so artfully and with such care and deliberation have been placed in that wicker basket in the kitchen. Windowpanes, cars and porches, these are important things, and maybe to a watchful or to a particular craftsman's eye they could be considered beautiful, but there is no natural beauty in them.

They are tainted by human hands, their mystery dissolved, or at least partly shielded by a simple, easily understood and identifiable human who has created such things through toil. The old Toyotas, although stoutly made and reliable, do not inspire wonder at some possibly all-seeing God. The glass in a window, though it may amply and without protest serve its designed purpose, does not cause one to pause for a moment to consider the mysteries of the world we live in, or to consider the origin and the significance of all life maybe, if I have not taken this thing too far, which is entirely possible. These things are seen too oft, and the succession of events in the fabrication of these manmade items is too long to trace them back to their more natural elements of silica, minerals and noble trees. That is too much consideration at once to beg the interruption of a human being's thoughts at just a mere glance, but a simple though miraculous Zucchini....

If this is what Ron thought, I should not pretend to know, but he saw something in those Zucchini for a week or two that fruitful summer, something that deserved a second thought. In the same way that they had grown from unassuming seeds and flourished, so too could the simple sight of them plant a thought in a contemplative mind, which, like the Zucchini plant, was capable of bearing fruit. If you visited the vine, now, to stare at the soil those Zucchini had once been rooted in, you would find nothing of particular interest, nothing that would point you to the cause of such creation, no explanation. I think the answer to this enigma correlates in some way to the fate of us all, the basis for our beings, the rationale of our goings. It all traces back to one simple mystery, to one unknown. Things of delicious mystery and things of importance need only the basics to commence: soil, sunlight, water, a seed. Then they may grow in the most complicated and intricate ways. In the midst of turmoil and chaos, which appeared so prevalent, those Zucchini would give remembrance to the things that really mattered, to the sanctity and precious wonderment of life, and so bring a troubled mind caught up in the manufactured hassle of the everyday back down to earth. And so the Zucchini earned their spot in the wicker basket, the showcase of the house for a spell. Ron, their spokesperson and guardian, vouched for their continued safety, which they had so richly merited that fateful summer.

We were all sort of ambling about the kitchen that day—Paul, Matt, Jer, Eben and I—a little restless and wondering what it was we should do for a little excitement. Suddenly Paul noticed that Scott was out in the yard, for what reason could not be keenly observed, but Scott's business was often too intricate and complex to be discerned at a glance. Like a mushroom, to look upon him was only to observe the surface, for you did not know what went on beneath. He was a man of ideas. Paul, acting on an impulse, and with a simple and understandable want for a little excitement, announced with the fervour of a warden in the middle of riot, "Lock all the doors!" As Matt and myself gazed around, a little bewildered, unsure of what the sudden urgency was all about, Paul madly dashed out of the room to fulfil his own orders throughout the rest of the house. Jer ran around and reeled in the many windows in the kitchen area. Eben stood there and didn't think the idea was a good one. Matt and I, still unsure if we wanted to be part of such a scheme, nonchalantly wandered over to the side door and fastened the lock, fulfilling a small, though integral, part of the overall plan.

Paul returned. At that point, all there was left to do was to bring it to Scott's attention that he was locked out of the house. We did this by staring out the window at him without saying a word—the recognized symbol of the land that something was indeed up. Scott started from whatever it was he was doing and took a few rapid steps towards the house. He tried one of the doors, probably knowing what he would find before he even touched the handle. He then stepped back onto the lawn to show that he knew what was going on and that he was not going to humour us by running around frantically trying other handles. The game of seeing Scott locked outside began to lose its lustre. He didn't really seem to care if he was outside or not. Before too long even I wanted to go outside, but that would have ruined the game. Looking around the kitchen for an idea, Paul remembered Scott's two Sarsfield's apple pies, the ones he had just bought, sitting innocently up on top of the cabinets, out of reach. It is an unspoken though vehemently enforced law that one should never eat food that someone else has bought or in some way laid claim to, at least not without permission. This law was both known and well understood by all of us, but where there is a law there is, of course, some small primal instinct and want deep down to break it, at least in someone. Why else the law? So Paul, having resigned himself to the fact that he was about to cross that line between law-abiding and the lawless, climbed up onto the counter and brought down the apple pies. He took one of them in hand and lifted it above his head in Scott's direction as though it was a goblet of wine, almost sombrely entreating Scott to wish him well on this journey he was about to partake in. And then, without further ado, he lowered the pie and, still standing on the counter, dug into it with a ferocity of appetite I am sure he did not feel in the physical sense.

Scott was livid. He raised his arms and pressed himself against the kitchen window, yelling, spittle accumulating on the pane. That was to be Scott's dinner; none of us had eaten much all day. What Scott said I don't know. He did not appear to be forming any actual words, but the intention was nonetheless well felt. Paul, Matt, Jer, myself, and even Eben, gazed down upon him through the window as though he was some wonderfully wild, vicious beast, the look in our eyes a mix of awe and fear. The panes of window acted like the bars at a zoo, keeping the animal safely away from us, but at the same time allowing us to observe him and so satiate our curiosity, but not without a faint touch of nervousness in the back of our heads about what might happen if such a creature were to somehow get out, or get in, as the case may be.

We watched Scott in all his fury for what may have been only a couple of moments. Then, it was almost as though we could see the idea dawn on his face. Scott stopped, hesitated, and then took off like a dart. We weren't sure where he had gone. We asked Paul if he had locked the back door of the house, and he said he had. We all stood around a little uneasily, unsure of what to do. Paul still stood on the counter, eating the pie a little more slowly, as though thinking. Jer just stood there watching. Absent-mindedly, he touched the crank on the window to see if it was secure. Matt and I turned and started towards the couch; Eben stood there and looked like he wanted to say something to ease the tension. There was silence as we waited—for what we did not know. Maybe nothing, but we figured probably something. All of a sudden we heard the sound of someone crashing through the house at such a speed that it was obvious they weren't stopping to move chairs and things out of their way. It had not taken long for Scott to figure out a way in. Startled, Matt and I hardly had time to turn around when the rapidly building climax of crashings burst through the French doors that led into the kitchen. Yelling, and with his arms flailing in every direction, Scott halted for a moment and Paul, still with pie in hand, wore an expression of both extreme fear and delight. Scott reminded me a little bit of the Tasmanian devil, with his flailing. Paul danced around on the counter out of Scott's way, half laughing, sending crumbs of apple pie cascading from his mouth, and half scared of his incensed brother, as though he could not decide which. Finally, in a defensive action, he threw the half-eaten pie at his brother, striking him in the head. This made Scott one of the most angry clowns I have ever seen. Madly glancing around, without thinking, he grabbed a hold of the two prized

 Zucchini and, with a draw that would have made Doc Holliday take a second look, in one fluid motion, sent them hurtling towards Paul. Paul, whose reflexes were just as quick, deftly dodged the two projectiles, but he paid for it by leaping onto the stove, whose elements were on. The Zucchini splintered on the cupboards behind him. Paul's feet were now on fire, and he jumped back off the element onto the counter. Somehow the scene escalated, and Paul and Scott were now both on the ground, holding kitchen knives, from where they got them I don't know, maybe thin air if you were to inquire about the room.

"Now come on, I don't think we should use knives," Eben said, being the most safety-minded, Matt and I looking at him wishing to point out that most of us did not even have any knives. He said this, but he said it with little conviction, like a sheriff in an old Western who tries to stop a fight, but knows he is vastly outgunned, so he only says something so it can be known that he did, and then steps back and sticks around so he can enjoy the show. It was around this time that the phone rang. Jer walked over to answer it, putting the index finger of his free hand in his other ear so he might more easily discern the voice over the racket of the yelling and manoeuvring of chairs.

This ability of Jer's to stay cool "in the thick of it" was a quality we much admired, and one that we all felt we possessed to the highest degree. There is never a good time to lose your cool, least of all at the height of the fray. It was the MacInnises' grandmother on the phone, just wondering how her boys were doing. Jer suggested that she might try and call back at a slightly later time, for right now there was a war going on, and with that he hung up the phone since he was having trouble hearing.

Paul was the underdog in this clash, being as that he lacked Scott's anger. Still, he knew how to counter, and like a couple of fencers they circled the kitchen table, scrutinizing one another for any small body movement that would signal an impending strike. It was not uncommon for situations between Paul and Scott to degrade into exactly what was before us now, and for some reason it always seemed a festive affair for Matt and I. We would jump around the extremely serious Scott and Paul, pretending we were having our own little fight, jabbing at one another and laughing. Scott and Paul would never even seem to notice us or our antics. We knew this was not going to be a real fight, because Paul was clearly in the wrong. You can't have a fight when one person is clearly in the wrong, unless something changes and the person in the right goes too far, which does sometimes happen.

This went on for a while, but the situation was eventually diffused in some more or less amicable way—maybe by some small, well-timed joke by Matt, Jer or me; maybe by the fact that pieces of Paul's socks were still smouldering on the element; maybe it was some sort of divine intervention; or maybe the humorous dashing of the Zucchini eventually brought things to a halt, its last great act, towards peace. Whatever the case may be, the excitement took a rapid decrescendo and whatever caused the peace to return has been overshadowed and forgotten by all the exhilaration witnessed only a few moments earlier in time, and so, on this point my memory fails me completely.

A sole pie remained, sitting on the counter, still half exposed in the Sobey's bag, seemingly innocent of the excitement it was capable of inciting. Scott later ate the remains of the other pie from the floor with his bare hands, in his own words "like a ravenous beast," not wanting a bit to go to waste. Afterwards, when thought returned, the events reminded us that even the most innocent and undeserved can get swept away with the sometimes vagrant notions and passions of humankind, too soon forgotten. Before long Ron would return; we'd have to lay low. The chunks of Zucchini were meticulously picked up, carefully reassembled on the counter, and tediously pinned back together using toothpicks, in the hopes that no one would ever notice. We did our best, but parts were lost, could not be brought back; it was imperfect, cracked, with edges, no longer smooth; we were no Gods, nor did we think we were.

8 *There's Only One Fishing Story*

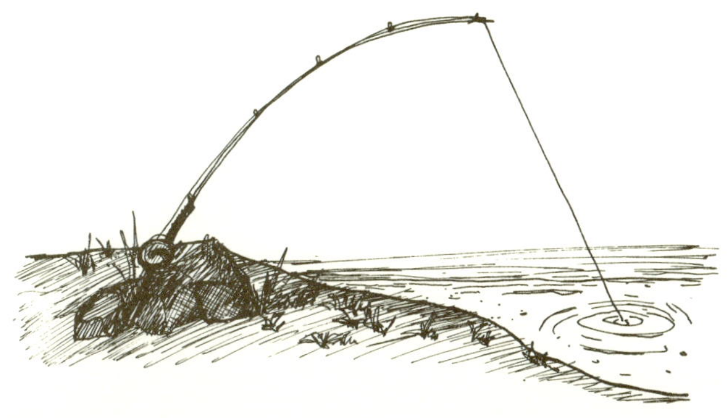

"You have to twitch the fishing pole like this," Scott said, gazing away from us with Matt and I looking on, slightly interested, but trying not to look it. Scott was moving his wrist, causing the lure to jump through the short grass in little intervals, making it look like a grasshopper coming along. Scott had given the lure a big cast out onto the lawn, Matt and I on the porch. Scott was on the lower of the two porch steps.

Scott continued to reel it in. "It makes the fish think it's alive." He paused. The hook was caught out in the grass somewhere. The end of the pole bowed right over. Scott pulled back hard, the rod bending right over his head to a near snapping degree. He pulled it pretty hard to the right, for a second, without much luck, and then when he pulled back to the left, the lure shot back as if out of a slingshot. Everybody ducked their heads a little as the lure flew over us and nailed the side of the house.

"Jesus," was all Matt said, and Scott smiled the way he does when there is a little danger in the air and he knows he has a hand in it.

"And that's how you get your hook unstuck," he said, trying to contain the smile.

Normally Scott could not have held Matt's and my attention with such a show, but the day before he had come home in his old Honda Accord with a live trout; the trout was in a little tin he had scavenged out of a ditch somewhere. The tin wasn't much larger than the fish. Miraculously the critter was still alive and Scott put it in the ornamental pond we had made off the porch, under the sumac trees, where the bees swarmed around the peculiar, fuzzy-looking flowers when the sun was out. This made Scott something of a fishing guru, although in those days it took very little knowledge or expertise to gain guru status. Our lives were characterized by a sort of pioneer mentality. The first person to try a particular sport was the guru of that sport, the first guy to have a girl was the guru on girls, and so on.

"I found a new place to go fishing," Scott had said the day before. "I only had my line in the water about a minute and I got that trout." This all had sounded pretty good. It usually only took about a minute before we started getting a little impatient and wondered where all the fish were, so this sounded like the sort of place we might like to fish at.

We had all been fishing several times before, of course, whenever the urge struck us, or whenever the urge struck one of us and the rest just moseyed along because we were bored. Sometimes we went fishing down by the Delhaven wharf and caught smelt, but usually after a while down there we would abandon fishing to walk around the beach and investigate the skate and the shells that the fishermen would throw overboard when they were sorting out their catch. Mostly though we would fish for the little darting trout in Pereaux River; we'd usually fish at the base of my parents' driveway, just around the first bend of the Hubbard Mountain Road, where the river was a bit wider. The river was really a creek to anyone who has seen a real river, but they seem to call it a river around here. We had all caught a few trout out of there, and one time in elementary school Scott had used his lunch box to catch one of the elusive minnows that swam there in the shallow parts. This was quite a feat. The minnows would sit there perfectly still and you could go after one with your hands or a bucket and be almost sure you had gotten it, only to find you had nothing at all. You hardly ever even saw them move, they just seemed to appear and disappear in the blink of an eye. In general, though, the fishing at the river was not great. Either the fish had plenty of better things to eat or they were onto us and knew not to go after shiny lures when people were running up and down the banks, knocking a little gravel in now and again, yelling to each other that they thought they saw something. You could easily go an afternoon and not catch anything. I guess that only made it pretty good when you did catch something though.

One of my earliest memories was of fishing in the

 Pereaux River. I had gotten a little yellow fishing rod with a red and white striped Devil brand lure, the kind you always saw. I was young enough that even though the creek was right at the bottom of my driveway it still seemed like a bit of an expedition just getting there. It was dusk and I sat on the big culvert, legs dangling, smelling the water and watching the water skippers. The river was flanked by swampy patches. The plants grew lush, and there were strange little flowers growing here and there. Once while walking through the swamp I stumbled upon a large single flower growing all by itself. The bloom was the strangest purple. When I tried to go back to find it I found I couldn't. Anyway, on this day I had asked my mother what I could use for bait and she had given me an orange peel. I took it, put it on my hook, and it was so big *I* couldn't have fit it in my mouth, let alone the little rainbow trout. I just sat there watching it; it didn't sink but sat there on the surface in the spinning current. After a while I stopped watching it twirl around and I just watched the water go by, the water skippers skipping, the trout darting, the faint mist that always gathered around the water at dusk. I listened to the little gurgling and the occasional snap of a twig out in the woods, and I thought about the strange purple flower out there somewhere, growing on a little mound of moss under the always living and dying alders. I never did learn to catch a fish with an orange peel. Mom didn't have to clean a fish that night either.

Scott, Matt and I decided we better go back to this place Scott had found while the fishing was good. We scrounged together a few poles and lures and took off in Scott's car, Scott and me in the front and Matt in the back. We stopped at the Pereaux Store to pick up some bobbers, because Scott had an idea they might be handy. They were thirty-five cents each, hanging on a cardboard display on the wall. While we were there we figured we may 's well pick up some penny candy.

In Scott's car, arms out the windows, fishing poles laid up between the seats, trying not to let the hooks get caught on things—especially ourselves—every once in a while eating a penny candy, but trying to save them, we drove along.

After driving for a while and going down a few roads we weren't too familiar with, Scott said, "Here it is," and he started to go off the main road onto a dirt one.

"Oh wait, no," he said and did a manoeuvre to get us back on the main road again. I picked up a couple candies that someone had just dropped on the floor and ate them. Thirty seconds later we went down another dirt road and then we were there. There was a little hydro station there. There were tons of these around the little waterways of Nova Scotia, most of them made during the Second World War.

It wasn't until we got out of the car that we realized we didn't have any bait. The next twenty minutes were spent running around looking for worms. The area was rocky; the soil was poor with a lot of slate. It was poor worm country. We clambered around and eventually scrounged together a couple dozen scraggily looking worms. As soon as one person stopped looking, we all stopped and went back to the river, not wanting to be catching worms when others were catching fish.

We each put a worm on the hook and spit on it because we had heard somewhere that fish were attracted to that. No one really knew if this was true or not. It was one of those things you might be unsure about, but it didn't hurt matters anyways, so you might as well be on the safe side of things.

We walked around and chose locations along the shore, each in accordance with his own fishing wisdom. We cast our lines in and prepared to wait. I sat down and pulled a little brown bag of penny candies from my pocket, placed it on a rock beside me, pulled one out and ate it. I noticed Matt was doing the same.

"Catch anything yet?" I asked him, already knowing the answer.

"Naw, you?"

"Naw … look at Winker down there." We called Scott "Winker" sometimes because of the way he used to unknowingly wink his eyes when he was younger, and since that was what his dad, Ron, called him. Scott gave his lure a great cast and then reeled it in rather quickly. He did this a couple of times. He then reeled his line all the way in, hooked the lure to one of the loops on his pole and ducked into the bushes. After some crashings and snappings he popped back out of the bushes twenty feet further down and cast his line in again most expectantly. I think Scott felt there was a little more pressure on him to catch a fish, to show us that we should have been paying closer attention when he was giving us fishing lessons earlier in the day.

At one point Matt and I noticed that Scott was reeling with his rod bowed over, like he had something big. Scott yanked on it quick and reeled like mad for a second, but then we all realized it was caught on the bottom somewhere. He pulled from either side, and nothing. Then he let out some line and walked down the shore a ways, and pulling from that angle he was able to un-snag it.

Then, again, there was nothing. Matt and I talked a little more. Scott was too far away to carry on a conversation, and gradually Matt's and my words petered out and I just sat. I thought about how much better the penny candies I was eating probably tasted than any fish I might catch, although probably not as good for you. I watched some flimsy looking mosquito-like insects flitting up and down just above the water, always on the verge of falling in. Some of them would land on the water for a bit and would have trouble getting free. I thought about how little my lure looked like these insects and I wondered if the fish ate them or not. I thought about the way the soil was good back on the Hubbard Mountain Road, but the fishing was poor, while here the soil was poor, but the fishing was supposedly good. I looked up at the power plant and I thought about power. I wondered how far it had to go before it was used. It seemed funny that this was the source of so many little things, so many little things that whirr, spin or go beep. And I was staring at the rock I was sitting on and thinking about the way sometimes—

"Whoa, hey now," Matt said, and it took me a second to remember we were fishing.

"What do you have there?" I said, even though I

 could see his line darting side to side in the water, which meant it was a fish. "Do you have a stick? Probably just a stick. Getting all excited over a stick," I said. Everyone knew it was a fish.

"Oooh, she's a fighter," Matt said, knowing I was just blowing smoke up his ass. Scott looked over and stared as Matt's fish was just getting to the shore, and while he was staring he was reeling his line in so fast that his lure was skipping along the surface. I put my pole down, put a rock on it and left the line in the water, then got up and went to see Matt's catch. It was a little smallmouth bass. I went and filled up one of the five-gallon buckets we had brought so we could take fish home and stock some of the ponds back on the Hubbard Mountain Road. We put the fish in it and watched for a moment. Matt and I turned to the noise of Scott crashing through the woods. A few seconds later he popped out next to us on the shore.

"I told you it was good fishing didn't I?" Scott came running over to look at the fish.

"I've seen better," Matt said, everyone understanding that he hadn't. Matt cast his line out again and Scott cast his line out right next to him so their lines were in danger of entangling.

"Jeez, Scott," Matt said, but Scott only grinned, not taking his eyes off his line. I walked over, took the rock off my pole and when I reeled it in a little I could hardly believe it. Through the line I could feel the distinct vibrations of a fish.

"Hee, hee, heeee. How's this grab you?" I said as I started reeling in the fish.

"No way," Scott said, and he ran over and cast his

line in next to me before I even had the fish out of the water. I put my fish with Matt's fish in the bucket, and Matt and I looked at them for a bit, sticking a blade of grass or a finger in the bucket every once in a while to see if they'd go for it.

Scott started thinking he had the unlucky fishing pole so he traded his pole with Matt's. Matt cast out and was reeling in on his new pole when the line turned into a big knot around the reel. For a second it seemed Scott may have been right about his pole being unlucky. Matt left the rest of the line in the water as he tried to undo the mess, but then—

"Oh, Jeez," he said. He clutched the pole with both hands, wide-eyed like he was about to take off from the shore. Sure enough he had another fish on the line and Scott ran over, his sandals slipping and scattering the slate, making what seemed like a lot of noise, and cast his line in over there, shooting for the exact same fish by the looks of it. It was around that time that I felt a real tug on my line and it was so tight that it just made a clicking noise when I tried to reel it in. The line was moving wildly all over the place and when it gave me a little slack I tried to reel it in as fast as I could. At one point the huge bass leaped out of the water and wriggled back and forth a good three or four times before it splashed back in again, something like you would see on that "Real Canadian Fishing Show." I had never experienced fishing like this and I wondered if God was in on the joke, because I had never caught a fish in such a spectacular way before. Scott was looking over and I could tell he was wondering if he should come back and cast his line in near me again. After a good long fight I found I had a bass of a few pounds at the end of the line, and we had to get another bucket of water to hold it.

"I am afraid this fish may eat some of those other fish," I said with a laugh. And on the afternoon went, one fish after another, Matt and I. The fish seemed to sense our moods and the less need we had of catching a fish the quicker they would jump on the line. Scott switched his fishing spot again and again. Sometimes you can do a thing better if you really only do it with half a mind.

Whenever Matt or I would catch one we would say to Scott, "Is this how you're supposed to do it? Like this?" giving the end of the line a couple of twitches, a bass already on the other end.

"I don't even know if I'll reel this one in," Matt said at one point. "May just leave him there for a bit, my reeling arm is getting tired." By the time we started getting hungry for supper, Matt and I had each caught six or seven bass, but Scott hadn't caught a one yet. I think he would have leapt in after a fish if he had seen one swimming by.

After a while Matt and I got tired of catching fish. We stopped fishing and just stood around the buckets looking at our catch, sticking a hand in the water now and again, and Scott had nowhere to run to anymore. The fishing was over. On the drive home Matt and I were loud and boisterous, as people are when they are doing very little thinking. If Scott was quiet it was only in contrast to the loud noises of Matt and I re-enacting how we had caught the fish and asking each other repeatedly if we had seen each other when we had caught a particular one. Scott would just sort of grin and give a little chuckle when he heard us going on—"I mean, did you see me when I got that one on the line down near the bushes and it was going all over the place and then it jumped in the air and hoo hee hee...."

So there it was. We were making fun of ourselves as much as we were making fun of Scott, I think. When we got home we let the fish go in the big pond where we swam, and over the years they grew to enormous sizes and turned into black shadows that often haunted the underside of the raft. We told everyone who asked about fishing that day, and even some who didn't. We told each other about it most of all, even though we were all quite familiar with the story by now. Mostly we just wanted to hear it again ourselves so we could have a little laugh.

"Remember how Scott kept running over and you caught that one when your line was all tangled even ..." and "yeah, just twitch your wrist like this." And with a start like that the story could be finished by anyone who knew, and everyone got a chuckle, there being several tellers and listeners. That is just the story of one fishing trip, but it's the story we mostly think of when we think of a fishing story, the story you get if you ask around. It doesn't even have too much to do with the fishing itself when you think about it. It doesn't have much to do with anything. We had gone fishing before, and Scott, Matt and I went fishing at the same place again plenty of times after. Later, Scott would catch just as many fish as Matt and I, but we don't talk about those times near as much, not near as much … there's only the one fishing story, and sometimes you can do a thing better if you really only do it with half a mind.

9 *Old Maples*

The swing hung from a colossal old maple; it swung out over the driveway. The maple was situated up on a steep bank, about ten feet above the driveway, and only a few feet away from it. There had been many a surprised driver in the past—people were never ready to see a boy go flying over their car. The grass and moss were worn away on the slope and the dirt was packed down hard around the swing from where so many people had come in for their landings. I remember at one point we had the idea of having two swings hanging from the same branch, so two people could swing at the same time. This idea turned out to be a disastrous one, but you live and learn, and we were learning. It was a particularly sunny day, just past suppertime, but none of us had gone in for supper. We were too busy going about our business. It was just too nice a day to go in. Once it got a little darker we thought we might.

Matt and I had tided ourselves over by eating some of the raspberries that grew wild down towards the bottom of the driveway. The wild raspberries always tasted the best. They were a staple in a boy's diet at that time of year. You would always see the biggest, juiciest berries in the middle of the tangle. They just sat there, reflecting the late-day sun, tempting someone to try and venture through their thick, thorny stalks to get at them. How hungry you were decided for you if you were willing to get scratched up a little to get at the rich fruit in the middle. Down by the raspberries you could smell the water and the duckweed from the creek. You could always smell that smell when you walked over the creek. The creek went through a culvert under the driveway. I always liked that smell. It smelled fresh, it smelled of life.

After having had some raspberries, and after tiring of aimlessly walking around, Matt and I decided we would go up to the swing for a bit. The swing never ceased to entertain us, at least for a little while. We headed down the slope to the maple where the swing was secured. There were a few maples that lined the driveway, amongst many other trees. Those trees seemed almost as old as the soft mountains that formed the valley. It would take a few boys to circle a trunk with their arms. When we got to the maple we were disappointed and surprised to see that the swing was no longer there. Scott was there and he had just taken it down. We wanted to know the meaning of this. The swing was a good piece of rope. It was about a hundred-feet long and an inch in diameter. A good strong piece of rope was a rare commodity. Next to the large healthy maple that the swing *had* been secured to, there was another equally large but dead maple, just slightly further down the slope. It had been dead for years, and really hadn't bothered anybody.

The maple was more of a skeleton now. The little branches had long since dried up and snapped off in the wind; all that was left were the bigger branches. These still stretched up and out over the driveway, still impressive, and still trying to hold on to some of the majesty they had held in life. On parts of the tree the bark had cracked and fallen off in large sections. These now lay around the base of the tree. Matt picked up one large piece of bark and smashed it on the trunk of the old giant. Where the bark had fallen off the sun had bleached the wood almost white. The wood had grown harder while it was dead. It was harder than that of a live tree, but at the same time it was more brittle. The old tree still did have some strength though. It would stand there for another age if you let it. The whole tree was covered in patches of turquoise-greenish lichen. I remember the lichen would turn a darker hue when it rained. You could also smell the tree a little more when it rained. It always had a smell though, not bad, it was just faint. You could really smell it if you picked up a piece of bark and smashed it over the trunk.

Scott had somehow commissioned the Corolla. (Maybe he had a few pieces of firewood in the back that needed to be moved and stacked. That was an old trick.) He had the car parked in the driveway a little ways down from the dead maple. He was taking the old tree down, he said. Scott figured the tree was a hazard, possibly dangerous to people driving up the driveway. That was Scott for you, always looking out for the welfare and safety of others. I figured the swing was probably more of a hazard, not that I thought anything should be done about it. When you swung out, you generally veered in a semicircle out from the tree. You could run down the slope a bit with the swing in your hand, until your feet would no longer touch. The speed of your runoff would govern how far above the driveway you went. A fast runoff would swing you out further and thus higher. It was not unheard of for a mischievous boy to plan his takeoff just right so that when a car was coming in the driveway he could lightly skip with his feet over the roof as he went whizzing by. This had been done just as often by Scott as the rest of us. If there happened to be any other boys in the back seat of the car at the time, this feat would always be done to their utmost delight and amusement.

Scott was securing the thick piece of swing rope to the back of the Corolla. He said his intention was to pull the branches of the tree down piece by piece until eventually only the massive and slightly less perilous trunk would be left. Scott had received permission to use the car from Ron. Although none of us were near the legal age of formally being allowed to drive a car at the time, we were nonetheless occasionally granted permission to use the car close to home. This would happen if and only if the purpose put forward was deemed a laudable one; some job or act which necessitated a car, and that it could be reasoned upon doing would be bettering the grounds and the establishment, and, in the eyes of us boys anyway, make the world an ever so slightly better place to live. Even though Ron was usually a more fruitful choice, it was well understood that if things in our plans went wrong, the consequences, mainly in the yelling and chasing department, would be more dire. It was dubious self-responsibility. There was a general understanding amongst us all that if anything too incriminating was to happen during one of our plans the best things for us to do would be to collectively squint across the grassy fields towards the protective woods and gullies of the North Mountain. There we would stop, collect our breath and hope we could outlast human memories. This in mind, Matt and I still thought it was a little sketchy that Scott had told Ron that he wanted to use the family car to pull down the old maple by way of a rope attached to the bumper. Permission was (strangely enough) seldom granted for such ill-conceived, although innovative, plans. I wondered if Scott had used some sort of ambiguously stated query on his father. For example, maybe Scott had said, "I would like the use of the car so I can more easily transport wood from one spot to another." Ron might have thought that Scott intended to transport wood from the pile out behind the barn to the house, whereas Scott was thinking more along the lines of moving wood from the top of the old dead maple down to the bottom. This is only conjecture, for Matt and I did not ask about the particulars of how Scott got the car. This was one of those cases where our sustained ignorance would actually act as a virtue instead of a vice. Matt and I figured since Scott had, of his own accord, received permission for the use of the car, then it should follow that the consequence for such mischief, should any happen to befall the vehicle, ought to land squarely on the car's temporary proprietor, leaving all other parties not present during the verbal contract entirely free of liability. In the back of our heads, however, Matt and I also knew that such legal particulars were not always adhered to, and that this was a sometimes lawless, live-by-the-seat-of-your-pants kind of land we lived in. The fairness of judges and juries could not always be counted on. Or maybe it was just that they were not always as familiar with the laws of the land as we were, meaning that we could not always rely on our arguments, which were filled with legal technicalities and judicial sleights of hand, to get us off.

Matt and I, weighing the facts over in our minds, decided that it would be prudent of us to at least lend Scott a hand in his work. The first branch he selected was way up near the top of the maple. He tied the rope around his body and climbed about thirty feet up into the old dead tree. He secured the rope to a branch not more than eight inches in diameter. He climbed back down, got into the Corolla and started it. Matt and I positioned ourselves a little ways back from the tree, but not too far, so that in all probability we would still have to run around dodging branches when Scott pulled on the rope. Scott eased down the driveway in the car. When the rope began to grow taut Scott put the car in neutral and allowed gravity to tighten it up.

The branch was keeping the car from rolling down the hill. Scott got out of the car leaving the door open and we all went to investigate the tightness of the rope. Just as we were doing so we heard a thunderous snap and a crack as the branch gave way. Scott ran back to the car to keep it from rolling. Because of the tightness and elasticity of the rope, the branch was propelled towards the car. Thankfully it fell just short. Scott got out of the car and we all just stood around smiling, looking at the branch that had been pulled out of the tree. We piled the dead wood off to the side of the driveway.

We did this several more times, laughing at the loud cracking noises the old branches would make. It almost seemed absurd, the noises were so loud. Occasionally we glanced up towards the top of the hill, towards the house, to make sure the noises had not gotten anyone's attention. We always chose a branch not much more than eight inches or so in diameter, and one of us would climb up there to tie the rope. We got pretty good at that, and before long we had really crafted "tree branch pulling down" into a fine art. But we needed to take this thing to the next logical level. It was obvious that all the good momentum of the car was being wasted by waiting until the rope was taut so that gravity and the weight of the car broke the branch. We decided we could probably take some bigger branches down if we got some good speed up, allowing the quick singing tightness of the rope to snap the branch. We tied the rope to a bigger branch. Scott headed down the driveway in the car. He drove fairly slowly but the added benefit of the car's momentum was soon obvious. It snapped the branch off with remarkable ease; however, the side effect of the added speed was that the elasticity of the rope became that much greater, and the dead branch flew towards the car that much faster. Scott, observantly seeing this, compensated by gunning the car as soon as the branch snapped free. Even then, the branch only narrowly missed the car. After deliberating on this fact we decided that gunning the car the whole way was the safest thing to do. If the branches were going to persist in flying after the car, we would simply have to outrun them. Again we took a lot of branches down in this manner. With much mirth we would watch the branches bouncing along behind Scott in the car after he had pulled them free. Sometimes Matt and I would sit in the back of the hatchback and look out the rear window to see how funny it looked to have the branches come hurtling towards us.

After a while this was just getting too easy again; it seemed as though the car could pull anything down. We started selecting bigger and bigger branches. The bigger the branch the more exciting it was when it came crashing down, and the louder the cracking noises. There were pieces of broken bark and debris scattered all over the driveway. Finally Scott selected a branch that was about a foot and a half in diameter. This was a fair bit bigger than anything we had tried thus far. To watch a branch of this size come crashing down was going to be pretty good. Scott got into the driver's seat. Matt and I decided that we would ride in the back hatch. We were going to need all the momentum we could muster. Scott really gave it this time.

We flew down the driveway at breakneck speed. Matt and I watched out the back as the rope on the ground was pulled along and up into the air. The rope began to tighten. Then there was a lot of confusion. We had underestimated that old tree, I am afraid. Those Toyotas were built tough, for it was not the tree that gave way this time, and it was not the bumper that gave way either. In fact, nothing gave way, although I think it might have been better if something had. In a flash we had gone from moving forward at a pretty good clip to moving backward at just about the same speed. That rope had a hell of a lot of spring in it. Instead of watching the branch come sailing down at us, Matt and I watched as we flew up towards it. The rope lifted the back end of the car, and I dare say even the front end a bit, right off the ground. The back bumper was probably about six or seven feet in the air. Matt and I were now looking straight on up into the blue sky. Because of the angle, and because the front of the car was much heavier than the back, its nose dragged on the ground. We ended up in a position that left us almost entirely balanced on the front bumper of the car. We hung there precariously for a moment. I remember turning around to look forwards through the windshield of the car only to find that it pointed directly into the sand of the driveway. After hovering there for a moment the car slumped over against the sandy bank that lined the driveway. Now it rested at an angle only slightly less vertical than before.

We were all a little dazed—but a small part of us, to tell you the truth, was not really all that surprised. Matt and I started to climb through an open window in the back seat. We were climbing out onto the sandy bank that the car now leaned against, its back end still way up in the air, when as though from the heavens, we heard a chilling voice. "Hey … what is going on?" We all just stood still, completely stunned, and listened, unsure of what we had really heard. We looked up the tunnel of a driveway from which the sound had seemed to originate. It was hard to see. The sun was setting. The angle of the sun and the angle of the driveway were aligned. The sun looked like the bright light at the end of the tunnel. It was a surreal feeling, hearing that sound and looking at that bright light. As our minds cleared and our eyes adjusted we could make out a silhouette way up at the top of the driveway. It was Carole, making her way down towards us. This was not a bright light that any of us wanted to walk towards at this particular point in time. Matt and I separated ourselves from Scott, secretly hoping this would have the effect of separating our previous actions from his, too. Like a couple of bunnies we scurried into the wild rose bushes and thick brambles which covered the bank. Those bushes seemed safe. I could see why the bunnies did this so often. We hoped we had not been seen, and continued hurrying as quietly as we could through the thick underbrush, gradually distancing ourselves from the scene, and from any consequences. Scott took off in another direction, but of course he was already implicated, through his possession of the car.

We never did head in for supper that night. It was best to just lie low for a bit at times like these. You know, let things blow over a little. At least, let them blow over as best they could. Sometimes things like that could only blow over so much. The car, it was all right. It did not take much for us to cut it down later. The skeleton of the tree remained standing for many more years. The small pile of dead branches at the side of the driveway stayed for a while as a testimony to our industriousness, though the trunk still proudly stood there, too, reminding us that we were only boys—and that compared to the vast powers of nature, boys we would forever be.

10 *The Trick*

It started out innocently enough, as devious things generally do. We were a bunch of boys with plenty of time on our hands. Idleness and an excess of time are dangerous things—fun things at times, but dangerous nonetheless. There is no telling what ideas will crop up in the heads of boys with little to do. The rest of the world was busy going about its business, adhering to moral codes, making deadlines, cultivating powerful acquaintances and dropping wounding ones. We were out back in the middle of pretty well nowhere, and that was where we wanted to be. There were no large buildings, stores, or flashy lights to entertain us, however, nor even many other people for that matter. The television only picked up one-and-a-half channels. The CBC would come in pretty good most of the time, but there wasn't really much on that that would interest someone younger. There was one other channel that we would half get every once in a while, but there was not much on that most of the time either. On the freak days when the reception was a little better we would sometimes watch it for a bit, just because we figured we better since it was on, and you never knew when or for how long it would be coming through.

So we had to provide our own entertainment. If left to your own devices you would be surprised at all the things you could come up with. I mean, maybe if you have a pretty hectic life, and all of a sudden you find yourself with a couple of free minutes, you might find it hard to think of something to entertain yourself with. You might get ideas like, "Hey, why don't I pick up this magazine and skim through it for a couple minutes. Ahh, a magazine," or "I always have been meaning to empty out some of those things I don't need in the glove compartment of my car," or finally, "Hey, I know, I'll take everything off my canned goods shelf and place it on the counter so I can really give the shelf a good dusting; that is something I can do. How the dust does seem to collect in there, yes, indeed." Occasionally, on our few excursions into the more populated regions of the world, we bore witness to people doing these very things, and perceived them with much wonder. What a very foreign way to think. I would never think of clearing a shelf so as to better dust it. I don't think I would even think of dusting a shelf. I never was partial to dusting, and may the dull time never come where the business increases in its importance.

Bugs and small critters in the house; they never bothered me much, either. For some people, though, a sowbug on the floor, a mouse or a chipmunk in the wall, is a cause for serious concern. Who knows what schemes that squirrel in the tree is contemplating as he eats seeds stolen from your bird feeder, keeping one darting black eye on you. Birds are generally endured because it's well known that they lack the ambition to be a threat ... except blue jays and crows. My point is that some people think differently. Maybe out in Pereaux some of us were a little wilder, had a wear-your-pants-three-days-in-a-row, tadpole-catching, ant-enduring, nose-blowing sort of approach. At any rate, there was no squirrel we lived in fear of.

It's relative, I guess. Our ideas were different and so was our idea of a good time. Sometimes days would go by without any good ideas. It's not like we had one after another, but we had quite a few. When you have a few boys sitting around idle in the middle of nowhere for an unlimited amount of time, you know eventually they are going to come up with some pretty good ideas for how to entertain themselves. (I am restricting my argument to boys here, for at the time girls were nothing but an unfamiliar passing curiosity.)

We had come up with plenty of ideas in our time, by our standards. One time we dug a hole. The hole grew and grew until we realized we did not know what we were going to do with it.

Another idea we had was to build a snowmobile trap in the wintertime. The snowmobiles always went over our property. They always seemed to go by the same routes—a trail I guess. We discovered that, for being the smartest animals on the planet, humans, especially those on snowmobiles, are about the easiest to trap. I think their downfall is that they think they are so smart that nothing would ever try to trap them.

Right now, though, I'm going to talk about one of our most infamous good ideas … some people still widen their eyes at the name. Some don't think it should be talked about, think it's better left forgotten. I'm talking about the Propane Condom Trick.

None of us were very old; we really did not have too much use for condoms as of yet. However, the MacInnises' mom was a caring sort, and she wanted to make sure she did right by her boys. When they were at a young age she gave them a talk about sex, and all the things she thought they should know about it. She even had a bunch of condoms and said that if and when they got themselves into that sort of relationship they should be sure and use them. Well, those condoms sat in a little basket up in the bathroom for sometime. None of us really had any occasion to use them. We were thinking though.

As we often did when we weren't actually putting one of our ideas into action, Paul, Matt and I were lounging around in the kitchen. Scott was strangely absent. We were just sitting around on the couch and chairs, talking a little, wondering if we should make ourselves something to eat, wondering if there was anything to eat, wondering if—in the case that there wasn't anything to eat—we should try and take steps towards finding something to eat, and finally wondering if maybe we should go play some baseball out in the field. This would give us some exercise and build up our appetites so that food would taste all that much better.

Suddenly Scott strolled in the door. That got our attention, at least enough for us to lazily look in his direction. Nobody really said anything. We were just looking over to see what was new with Scott—we were always interested to see what was new with people—even though we had just seen Scott only half an hour ago. Now he had a condom and a small tank of propane in his hands. He said he had found out something we could do with the condoms.

The sight of the condoms still made us laugh a little. I already had a good idea of what Scott's plan was. I can't remember if Scott told us to gather around, or if nothing was said and it was just something that we instinctively did. Scott filled the condom up with propane, shut the tank off, and then placed the tank on the ground. He pinched the condom closed. He opened up the stove and placed a stick in the coals so that the end of it would light. He pulled out the stick with a little flame burning on the end. Scott was standing on the semicircular arrangement of bricks, in the corner where the stove sat, a place where many small pyrotechnic displays had taken place. He put the end of the condom up in front of the flame, and released the propane that he had been pinching off. There was a spectacular fireball. We all knew exactly what was coming, but we still all delighted in the flame. I'm not sure why a huge fireball is such a great thing—the lighting, the flash of heat, the hint that there may be a little danger. I think it might be the danger. Danger makes a lot of things more exciting.

After seeing this I recalled that a few years ago there had been the Propane Balloon Trick. This trick was very similar in nature to the Propane Condom Trick; I guess it was only due to the fact that we were older now that condoms were now used instead of balloons. The problem with the Propane Balloon Trick had been that balloons were really a bit of a rarity around these parts. No one ever had too many balloons on them, and nobody was supplying us with balloons. With the arrival of condoms in the house this was no longer going to be a problem.

After Scott had given us his little demonstration, the Propane Condom Trick became a regular attraction, an old standard. I am not sure what Carole was thinking. She must have been rather surprised at the number of condoms we were going through, but maybe she was just glad that we were all being so safe. Any guest that came over requested the Propane Condom Trick, and we were only too happy to oblige. For the most part it was Scott who put on the actual show, leaving the rest of us to sit around with knowing grins, exchanging looks and nods, watching the guest in anticipation of the surprised look that would appear on his face when the huge fireball lit up the room; but the guest could just as easily be a "her"—a huge fireball was one of the few ways we really knew how to communicate with a girl back then. This look was made all the more enjoyable by the dazzling light of the fireball reflecting off his or her every feature and sparkling in his or her eyes. This was the moment we all waited for and enjoyed. That look became the whole reason for the Propane Condom Trick.

This series of fiery exhibitions went on for several weeks. Like I said, it was mostly Scott who did the actual trick, but occasionally one of us would give him a rest on a night, and quite often we'd assist him by holding the flame in front of the condom or something of that nature. Like all good entertainers we knew that we were only ever as good as our last show. Each time we did the trick we had to make it bigger, flashier and more extravagant than the last to keep the people coming back. It's a dangerous creed. Like the daredevil stunt-bike jumpers that were so popular back in the sixties and seventies, we had to keep taking it up a notch. The stunt-bike men used to add more barrels, or cars, or jump over a gorge or something. We kept adding more propane. It was the only way. We had to give the public what it wanted, or maybe it was what we wanted; we were hooked on the adrenaline that only a professional daredevil showman knows; we may have even been a little deranged by it.

I think it was me—although it always seems that way after time has passed—who first noticed a curious side effect of the trick. After we had increased the size of the fireball considerably, there was, only hardly perceptible at first, a small compression wave caused by the rapidly ignited gas. At first, the pressure change was only slightly noticable on your skin and in your eardrums. I believe it was the same sort of compression wave that results from the detonation of bombs and things of that nature. It was the sort of thing that you see on those famous old videos of nuclear tests—the ones where you see the compression wave literally blowing a house apart, or flattening trees right to the ground, or sending a jeep flying. Of course the compression wave I am talking about was nowhere close to that scale—but at the same time I guess it deserves to be in that category. Until I noticed this, I had never really placed the Propane Condom Trick in the same category as bombs and things of the like, hadn't realized we were playing with fire, not the kind you saw in those old films anyway, or the kind known to bring down whole cities.

At first it was easy to doubt your senses, the feeling was so faint. When the fireball went off you were too preoccupied with the show in front of you to really try and concentrate on the slight, almost unperceivable, pressure on your skin and eardrums. But not long after this we were given concrete evidence, something that undeniably pointed to the existence of a compression wave that travelled throughout the room and who knew how far if given the liberty. In the beginning it was just a noise. Our backs were turned so we didn't know what had made the sound. A rattling was heard at the far end of the room. The next time we did the trick we realized what the sound was. Just after we lit the propane off, the French doors on the far end of the kitchen, about twenty-five feet from where we were, rattled with the impact of the wave. This seemed sort of funny to us at first. Having the door rattle added to the trick. It was a testimony to the power of the fireball we were creating—the one we commanded, the one that obeyed us. On subsequent demonstrations we would even draw our audience's attention to the French doors, putting them on the ready for the phenomenon that was sure to happen. This trick was only getting better. To be sure that the rattling gave the desired effect we had to increase the amount of propane even more. Once we did this there was no missing the movement of the doors. Now, instead of rattling, there was a very perceptible bowing of the double doors in and out, and the pressure upon the skin and ears was no longer faint, but definite—similar to the feeling one would get driving down the mountain. It was almost becoming violent at this point, but we were still in control, we gave the orders.

None of us were worried. The trick continued on. It seemed to grow bigger, more dazzling, more brilliant, every time we performed it. It may have started to take on some life of its own. It had to keep getting bigger. That is just the way it was. After we had seen the trick once, it was old news. What we wanted to see now was the same trick only bigger. Of course this need for it to continually grow bigger came from Scott, Paul, Matt and I, for we had witnessed every show. The people who had seen the show in the beginning did not get near the show that it was to become in the end. Of course when word got out that it had become bigger, had changed to something more strange, there were a lot of people coming back to see it again.

With all things, both good and bad, there must be an end. The last demonstration of the Propane Condom Trick is burnt into my mind. It was the grand finale, the show to end all shows. It had to be, it had evolved into something we merely let free; it got to the point where it was it or us. There was Scott, Paul, Matt and I, the witnesses to the birth and evolution of the show. Then there was Jer, a big fan of, and witness to, many shows. And finally there was Kelly, a first-time spectator and new arrival to the demonstration. For some reason, and for the first time ever, we decided to do the show up in Scott's room. Scott's room was a fair bit smaller than the kitchen downstairs. Maybe we did it up there because we figured the fireball would be that much more impressive if it filled up an entire room. Imagine a whole room completely filled with fire. Up to this point the flame had always been so quick that it did not burn anything much, so we were not too worried about the heat of the flame. By this point, not only had the production grown in the amount of propane used, it had grown more complex and scientific in the manner in which it was conducted. Scott had constructed a system in which the grotesquely inflated condom was held on the end of a long stick. Through some guides, clasps and a piece of string, he was able to rig it so that he was able to release the propane from a safe distance. Like I said, the fireball itself was not really all that hot. For some reason, the flame burned a little hotter right where it came out of the condom, and thus was a little more feared and respected. Of course someone still had to light the gas as it came out. For this demonstration Paul volunteered to be the lighter. The lighter had by far the most dangerous job. He had to be closer to the origin of the flame than anyone, although thankfully the fireball usually shot out and away from him. Because of the way the propane was forced out of the condom, the fireball usually started at the condom and then fanned out in whatever direction the condom happened to be pointed.

So Scott was holding, Paul was lighting, and the

rest of us got into position. Because of the amount of propane we were using, we knew that we were pushing the envelope, so to speak. The rest of us deemed it a laudable idea this time to seek refuge from the flame, for in this small room it was sure to engulf us. Matt sought out the closet, leaving the door open a crack for viewing purposes. Kelly, Jer and I sought shelter under a mattress, with only our eyes peeking out. We figured if things were to get too hairy we could easily duck under completely. So everybody was ready and in their places. We were quiet with anticipation. The single bulb that hung from Scott's ceiling dully lit the room, leaving shadows in the corners. It was time.

Paul held up the special barbecue lighter, giving him about a foot's distance from the flame, and Scott pulled on the string, releasing the propane. A fireball, the likes of which we had never seen, immediately filled the room. Matt closed the door so that only a sliver was left to look through. Jer, Kelly and I ducked underneath the mattress, but the flames still licked and curled all around it, seeking us out. Every corner and crevice of the room was dazzlingly lit by the huge flame. The light of the hundred-watt bulb hanging from the ceiling was completely eaten up by the great luminosity of the burning gas. This was a spectacle of spectacles. We were enchanted with the fear that this time maybe we had finally gone too far; we had unleashed something we could not control, that sought to form our destinies against our will and not the other way around. Maybe this time was it. There was overwhelming confusion, delight and fear. The pressure was intense, our hiding places seemed futile, we were found. We had lost control of this thing; I realized maybe not even that night, but days, maybe weeks before. It had known .... Just as it was reaching its peak and something had to give, a shattering sound ripped through the air, even faster than the burning gas had. There were no French doors twenty-five feet away in this room. The single door was shut and secured tight. It had to have something. The compression wave was much greater this time with the smaller room and the increased amount of gas. It had found a better way to get out of the room. At least I guess it decided to leave, and not stay. I'm not sure what would have happened to us, what it would have done to us, if it had stayed. As it left the room, the compression wave blew the windows out. Scott's room was on the second floor; the pressure of the thing escaping sent shards of glass flying from the room, landing across the driveway nearly forty feet away. Like a bunch of gophers we cautiously emerged from our hiding places and exchanged bewildered looks. The ethereal darkness, cool air and smells of the night seemed to seep in from the large holes where the windows had been. Again, only the single dim light bulb lit the room, and for a moment things were eerily quiet. We sat stunned for a moment, then someone noticed that Scott's stereo was very softly playing "Land of a Thousand Dances." We cranked the song up; it was too late for regret. Everyone danced around, energy stemming from the euphoria of making it through such an event, from surviving unscathed. The flame, like a bear, had sniffed us, but decided we weren't worth it and carried on. And that's what happens when there are no wars or calamities; a person begins to seek them out, throws stones and hides and peeks out when they think things are safe.

Not too much was said of the Propane Condom Trick after that, for the most part. I cannot recall how we explained away the missing windows—but you can be sure it was some long vague story laying most of the blame on the age and thinness of the panes. It really didn't seem necessary to include "Propane Condom Trick" or the flame in the explanation at all. Scott replaced his windows with garbage bags he taped up there. They stayed for several months, through the wintertime, till we could finally find a way to replace the glass. On journeys like these you are forced to make your own ends, for there are no real ends, and you have to concede when you are willing to go no further, draw a line between wisdom and pride. For some that is a dangerous thing to be left to do. We didn't try the trick again. We had seen all we wanted to down the road of the Propane Condom Trick, and we decided it was time to make our way back. Although occasionally, there's still that faint urge to throw a stone and hide.

11 *Farewell Pheasant*

I don't feel like reading, don't feel like watching television, though I guess that would be an easy way out. Don't feel like much of anything, but sitting here on the couch looking up and out the window at the leaves hanging on the maple tree branch outside. I don't feel bad, I don't feel good, I don't feel like answering questions about how I'm feeling. My thoughts are here and there, mostly there, sometimes concentrating really hard on something and going over a point in detail, as though afterwards I could check it off on a mental list I have going, like a chore I only wish to get out of the way and done. Other times I am just staring, out at the maple leaves, making a slight effort just not to think at all.

I hear the sound of gravel under rolling rubber coming down the Hubbard Mountain Road, then footsteps in the room next to me, moving towards the window. Through the closed door I hear my mom say (I have excellent hearing, almost a curse at times I feel) “Who is this coming down the road now?” Some more footsteps and I hear one of my sisters say, “I think they’re turning in … no, no maybe not. A blue truck. Who do we know in a blue truck?”

“I don’t know,” my mom says, and I can tell from the lack of footsteps that they are still looking after it, and I know from familiarity that there is a trail of dust in the air from where it went, growing lighter and lighter as you look down the road from where it came from, where the dust has had more time to dissipate and settle. Maybe they are looking at that right now. The mind is sometimes welcoming of something simple like that to take in, something to keep your mind from making lists that need to be mentally checked off, something to keep you from that slight effort it takes not to think at all.… In the next room over, though, with the door closed, I don’t look up. If I had any urge to lift my head so as to look out the window to solve the riddle, the small commotion caused in the other room from the truck down the road makes me kill it; the fact that the sound and the talking about it disturbed my quietude and my staring blankly out the window, and because all the commotion and distraction irks me at the moment, makes me kill any instinct to do so. There is no way you would catch me looking after a truck right now, trying to guess whose it was. Maybe some other day, when I act too quick to think about what I am doing, saying something like, “Hey yeah, doesn’t so and so have a blue truck?”—not even completely sure about my words really, just puttering along through life reacting to things, giving a few remarks here and there. But not right now, while I am thinking about it, while pheasants and things are dying all over the place and questions of blue trucks seem monotonously ridiculous and of no consequence—not while there is so much thinking, healing and mental listing to be done. I hope that pheasant is dead now, died quickly, but I don't know. It bothers me that people are worrying about the blue truck. Why worry about anything?, I think. I sometimes don't understand. I guess you have to; same reason you'd pull your hand out of a fire. Rationally, deep down, I think I still know this, somewhere. Same reason we all keep moving along. There's something to it, there's something there even if I am not sure of the particulars, a point on the mental list destined never to have a check by it, that will always have to be gone back to and gone over time and time again.

Things quiet down, light footsteps slip quietly away from windows, and my thoughts can again grow louder, concentrating in on myself while looking out—my eyes fastening to the tree outside again without really seeing it, so as to steady my thinking, the same way you would use your arm to steady yourself against a wall if you were tired, trying to recoup. I think about the day that has passed, running it over. Death has a way of stirring you up, making you think and question, especially when it taps you on the shoulder, even if it is only to ask the time.

Just this morning I had sat on the back step in the early sun, warming up like a turtle, smelling the lily of the valley planted by the walkway, the poisonous leaves hiding the little white bell flowers. I saw Sally the dog coming down the gravel road in the distance.

 She looks something like a black lab, with a white underbelly that makes me think she might be wearing a little fur tuxedo—pretty dressed up to be out on the farm, and somewhat comical to think about when I see her rolling in something. Sometimes she greets people when they go to church, whether they want to be greeted or not—quite a social dog.

"Who's that big dog?" I said, as though I had never met Sally before, as though she doesn't come every morning. My acting is never lost on Sally. Her quickened pace and tongue-hanging smile told me that she was. From the way she jumped around I knew she could tell I was joking with her and she liked it. Like people, sometimes she delights in being able to be ridiculous. I guess there is something freeing in being ridiculous; the same way you don't care if you don't win if you weren't really trying in the first place. The same principle applies for escaping into the half-ridiculous. People do a lot of talking without words; dogs sometimes understand this other language quicker than people do. I walked over, and although she is a big dog I picked her up like I always do, and she lay there like a puppy, flattered at being treated so young, her ears so soft. Sally, the sun, the step and flowers; that is how the day all started.

Life and death, joy, fear of dying, why people do it. People don't like to hear about it too much. People are tired of it. If someone mentions it you get a "here we go," even if it is only in people's eyes, and I know I give that "here we go" as much as anybody. Some say there is no known reason, others will gladly peel something off for you, showing you how together they have it. Even when I think about it I sometimes give a "here we go" to myself.

Back sitting in the room with the door closed, I hear the sound of the doorknob being turned, and all the sounds that go along with the door opening up—the bolt sliding across, it popping open, the creaking—it all seems so loud. My mind is all over the noise, right on top of it; I hear it completely, painfully clear. My mom walks in the door. I am looking at her because I heard her coming. She looks at me and says, "It seems someone left their socks in the middle of the floor out here."

"Oh yeah … was it you?" I say, venturing into the ridiculous a little, if only to make myself smile, my mom and myself both knowing that the socks are my own. She leaves with an "I don't think so." Not angry, but obviously having run into this sort of humour several times before and knowing how to deal with it. For a moment my thoughts drift away from the pheasant and pheasant-related thoughts, but not far. A couple of socks seems like a lot to open a door for, I think. I remember seeing socks several times throughout my life and I never once even bothered to go tell anyone about it. Everyone is different with what they concern themselves with. I guess my thoughts are no less trivial for the most part. But for the sake of thinking, in relation to pheasant and pheasant-related thoughts, why worry about a pair of old socks or where they are? It is one of those things that I wouldn't think to talk about, at least not in my current state, not at the moment. It would just seem strange coming out of my mouth. Like around the supper table one night, a little bit of food in my mouth as I talk, nonchalantly, raising my voice a little louder than usual to begin with, like people do when there is a group of people, no one is talking and they think they are initiating a real conversation that people will want to jump into. "So anyways, I saw these socks earlier today...." I can just imagine people looking on, half interested, waiting for the rest of the story, and me knowing they are waiting, but letting them wait, like I think I really have something for them here but before I continue I want to tease them a bit with the suspense. "Smack dab in the middle of the floor," I would finally conclude. After a couple "ohs" and "wells" as though this is what they were waiting for: "Yeah, right in the middle ..." I would say again, repeating that part as though it was the punchline or something, milking that part for all it was worth, and looking on as though there were any number of ways to respond and jump into that sort of dialogue and take it away from there, take it all away. I don't know where I could take something like that from there, but I have heard conversations almost like this all the time. Maybe not quite like this, but the formula is right. It's almost eerie if you think about it too much. People occupy themselves with such talk all the time. I rarely know what to say around the supper table, or in other places where you are expected to carry on such as this, but this trait of mine intensifies when I am thinking about things like pheasants dying, and related pheasant-death thoughts, when your thoughts are too far from that freeing, self-depreciating ridiculous.

When they're not thinking, I find, people have so many words flying out of their mouths that they hardly know what to do with them all, or what order to put them in. Sometimes I almost believe it's like a cricket chirping, a cow mooing, or a dog barking. I know even for these animals these sounds can have meaning, but nine times out of ten they don't and they are just making "noise for the sake of noise" as my mother used to tell me (and not in an encouraging way) when I would walk around the house with a stick and a pot singing a song, no words, only to be heard, to let people and things know I was there when I was much younger and didn't know how to make the appropriate kinds of noise for the sake of noise. A lot of the time people talk and the words aren't important; people just talk to let you know they're there, as a comfort, like a puppy curled up with a ticking clock, the sound of the tick taking the place of its mother's beating heart. This is living though. A lot of living is done through talking and interacting in such ways with others, the words sometimes jumping out as unconsciously as a blink of an eye, a scratch of an itch. Talking, like this around the table, is what people do, how people live, when they aren't thinking of pheasants or such things. People go to sleep and they wake up in the morning planning to do a little more.

I know I do this sometimes; I remember once consciously, I made a mental note of it, that this was what I had done. I was with my family and we were having salad as part of supper and I was eating out of this wooden bowl with a knot in the wood (the supper table being a great place to find such conversational examples). You could tell the bowl I had from all the other bowls in the set because of this darker brown knot in the wood, which none of the others had. It seemed to me that I always got the one with the knot in it. Not that it made any difference, it wasn't any better, or worse for that matter, but after considerable reflection on my part, and after noticing that no one else in the family was saying much that evening, I decided to say something, as though I was somehow doing my part—as though I had to fill the air with some words, make a little of the appropriate noise for the sake of noise, to wake us all up to the fact of life. Just in case God, who may be looking down on us, forgot that we were here and was about to put the earth in his closet and forget about it unless he heard a little noise, a little life. I rarely had this feeling for the need of a little conversation and the fact that I had it made me chuckle, so I pursued it to see where it would take me, although I admit I was leaning towards the half-ridiculous.

"You know, I always get this same bowl with the knot in the side of it," I said. "When we used these bowls a couple of weeks ago, I had it then too …. Never said anything about it at the time though …" I said, trailing off and lowering my voice as though it really didn't matter much to me if I was heard and understood or not. I took a bite of salad. "Yeah …." I dragged the word out, as though that would be the end of it unless someone else decided to jump in. And so that was out there, hanging in the air and people's ears for a moment. People hesitated, with forks halfway to their mouths, thinking about this, exercising their brains with it as there was nothing else directly in front of them to amuse their minds with, no still maple tree branches with leaves on them to steady their thoughts with. It took a while for me to get across to everyone what I was talking about, but I did. Some expressed doubt, some intrigue, others suggested answers venturing into the realm of psychology and probability, others philosophy. But everyone mulled it over, if only for a couple of minutes. I guess that's the sort of thing one talks about a lot of the time: knots in wooden bowls, strange trucks driving down the road, and the last time you saw some socks sitting in the middle of the floor somewhere.

It sounds like I am making fun, but think about it. If you're not asking the standard day-to-day practical questions such as asking someone where you left something you've lost, how their health is doing, what work they did or have to do, the latest gossip on what so-and-so has done or is doing, whether they think it is going to rain that day, or a few other odds and ends, you are talking, philosophizing, and speculating about old socks, knotty bowls, or mysterious blue trucks. Maybe other people have better stories, romances, gripping adventures. I guess I have one or two of those too, but they are sparsely strewn about between things like working, knots in bowls, socks in the middle of the floor, and mystery blue trucks. And most of this talk, no matter how gripping, eventually boils down to noise for the sake of noise, or the comforting tick of a clock, when thought about in comparison with the grand scheme of things, and our minds can just trail off incomprehensively when we think of the grand scheme, trail off with relief. Hardly ever do you talk about what you think about while steadying your thoughts on a maple leaf: the unquestioned fact of our existence, often forgotten; what people are running around for, assuming what they do is somehow important; of ponderings and the nature of humankind, of mystery and things like the ski ramp you made out in the gully last winter and the events connected to that, old Mr. Crowe in his sixties taking a header off the ski ramp, but jumping right back up like one of the boys. This talk is rare, like a lunar eclipse, or an unusually high tide. Certain kinds of people try to force this talk too much, out of order, and they have to lie and float around ungrounded and unwarranted, but wishing for something, dreaming, and you roll your eyes and grow tired of it fast and give them a "here we go" look. It's like it touches a sore spot you'd rather not aggravate until it has healed a little more, until you're a little stronger. Naturally occurring though, this sort of talk is rare, yet healthy and refreshing. Sometimes it crops up around a campfire in the woods, away from your job, house, the structure, with a few beers to free your tongue and inhibitions .... In a world with pheasants dying and everything else, you start wondering what makes it all important, and that is a whole other bag of beans.

Some say technology is important and progress is important, whatever the hell that means, as though every generation is more intelligent and superior than the last. They point at things like their cars and their VCRs, even though they don't know what goes on under the hood, or why their VCR flashes 12:00. Morally or ethically, I can't say I think people ever change. We collect technology every year, collect information; we collect things that glitter like gold, silver and rubies and shiny bits of information and pass them on. The whole world has this collection of shiny baubles and figures, but we're no smarter. It's like the stamp collection a grandparent gave you and you added a couple stamps you happened upon, too. Of course, many people will say that this is all important because *people* are important, or that we live for our children, but the cyclical errors that come from this are soon obvious. Is it important for me to live and carry on unknowing so that future generations can? And I do this for the generation before? Some people will stop arguing with you after you get to people and the children, and say that is the end of it and that you shouldn't question things any further. They are insulted, maybe personally, maybe scared, as though it were a sin, and it might be depending on who you ask. As far as I have discerned so far, people are important for making other people and also because who would you point out a pair of socks sitting in the middle of the floor to, or make a clever remark about a wooden bowl to, if there weren't other people around? This is as far as I have ever gotten. And science doesn't help me, it just clutters the equation with a bunch of variables I found later could be isolated and cancelled out. Maybe religion, I don't know. I'll probably only get stares the next time I try and turn this idea into idle conversation, sitting around a table.

These new thoughts have woken me up a little again as I sit here on the couch, and my mind swings, back and forth, from dark thoughts to half comical ones. I begin to recall more of the day, living things over again, checking off the list as much as I can.

As the morning progressed I puttered around for

 a little while and then I hooked the sickle bar mower to the Massey Ferguson. The sickle bar mower runs off the power takeoff and it hangs to the side, a bar seven-feet long with serrated blades that move back and forth with a quick lethal clicka-clicka sound. Some people think it is a good mower and some people think it isn't worth the powder to blow it to hell. And sometimes it depends on the mood you're in, or how much noise for the sake of noise a person figures the day warrants. Sometimes, if a couple of people are talking about something like that, it depends if one person is trying to guess at what to say so as to be in agreement with the other. Or sometimes a couple people will discuss it in an argumentative manner, a bit of a mock argument, talking loudly, both on the same side of the thing, getting themselves all excited, and carrying on while an imaginary contrary person stands there silent in a most satisfying way.

Sally the dog helped me hook the mower on as best she could with what she had to work with, neither of us thinking of pheasants or death yet. What she mostly did was sniff around everything, especially things I was interested in or touching, and occasionally she came over to look up at me when she wanted to be patted. Sally never had any clever remarks or anecdotes, only occasionally clever noises, and I thought my time with her was all right, so who knows, there must be something there. Sally and I could just sit there and ponder our own thoughts, and I amused myself with thinking that Sally sometimes thought the same things I did, a kindred creature that sits there silent in a most satisfying way. The company is nice I guess. I don't know why, and most of the time I don't think about it and don't even like to, I better stop.

I started the little Massey tractor, drove out of the barn, and the diesel puttered along up to the field, Sally jogging along beside. In the truck I had clocked Sally at fifty kilometres an hour one time, bad leg and all. There's a story for around the supper table; there's a reason for Sally to come over to be patted. As I approached the field Sally got bored and went off exploring. I was glad because I didn't trust her around the mowers, especially the sickle bar which is invisible until it's on you, and I have heard plenty of horror stories about that kind of mower. You can't even see the blades as they do their work a few inches off the ground, the grass falling after them. I started around the field, leaving smaller and smaller rectangles of grass standing. It was August, really too late for pheasants to be sitting on nests with eggs. The pheasant is a funny animal—their familiar call, the beautifully coloured large males, the females a dull brown and whom you can't see when they stand completely still in the grass, which they often do. There is nothing that can scare you like a pheasant either. They can scare the hell out of you. They always stand still, that is their defense. A few times I've been out walking through the tall grass of a field in the middle of the night, walking along in the complete dark and silence, and then, from almost directly under my feet, would come the startling screeching call and the loud buffeting of the wings as the pheasant powerfully beat them in its escape, taking off, and the sudden sound would almost beat my heart out. The MacInnises and I all have that same story, just different times and places. It'd be hard to tell them apart.

I sat on the Massey, my elbow on the red fender, staring, mesmerized, at the grass as it fell down neatly. I continued on like this for some time, the falling grass taking up my thoughts, round and round the field, smaller rectangles. Then there was a puff, a brown puff floating up, within the neat rows of grass falling neatly, only not so neat. I perked up, took my forearm off the fender and continued on, not sure what I had seen, looking back. What the hell was that? I thought. I continued around the field some more; before I got back around I realized what it might have been. Now I thought I knew, hoped I didn't. Once I got around again I saw it, the pheasant; its feathers all puffed up, sitting there, afraid. It must have been a younger pheasant. Only a younger pheasant would still be sitting on a nest of eggs in late August. It was probably an egg a year or two ago itself. I drove past the pheasant a little, thinking what to do, the clicka-clicka sound the background noise to my thoughts, as though it kept the beat, still mowing.

Then along came Sally—coming at me running, right for the falling grass, the blade, unknowing.

"Sally!" I heard myself say. But she came faster. Then again, "Sally! … SALLY!" and finally she stopped. "For Christ's sake get the hell out of here!" I raised my arm as though I was going to throw something at her, my fear for Sally quickly turning into anger, the sharpest emotion, quick to understand. My anger hit Sally and through the look in her eyes it hit me right back, her look of hurt and confusion. She jogged away, head low, tail low. I was mad I hit the pheasant, I was mad I yelled at Sally. I turned the tractor off and sat for a second, my thoughts confused and drifting, faster, slower, without the steadying clicka-clicka. I got off and strolled towards the pheasant. A quick turn of the pheasant's head towards me told me it was still alive. I saw that it was about three feet off its nest, sitting on the ground, fluffed up and looking big, trying to look bigger. There were about nine large eggs the size of a chicken's in the bare nest, brown specked, now red specked too. I also saw that the pheasant's legs and thighs were still sitting on the eggs, separate from the bird; it never moved. I had heard of this happening before, from other people who use this sort of mower. Next year there is no way I am mowing till September, I thought. Sure, people hunt all the time, but not like this, and I don't like hunting much anyways and we don't allow hunting on the farm. We like the pheasants, hundreds of them—soon to be less one, less ten if you are the type to count pheasants before they are hatched. The farm is really a haven for these birds. That is, if you can have gruesome sicklebar deaths and still call it a haven. I knew I had to kill this bird now. I didn't know how. Stomp on it? Maybe I should get a stick? That would be too far away. I'm in the middle of a field. I mulled these things over as I approached the scared bird; I wanted to make this quick, like sailing out over the gully on the aerial runway. I couldn't think too much.

Maybe you don't like hearing this, think it's tasteless, like someone talking about something disgusting while you are trying to eat. It would never be suitable for around the dinner table, but when is a good time to tell someone this kind of story? People always seem to be around the proverbial dinner table when it comes to such stories. Maybe this is something that should never be talked about. Something that should be consciously forgotten, something that should be ignored—pretend like these things don't happen, glaze over them with the ridiculousness. I sort of just plopped this story down like a sack of crap. Like the people who actually buy a sack of crap at the garden centre. Yeah, I've seen them. And the guy who brings it out to their car usually says, "So, where do you want it?" and then plops it down wherever. Stories like this are not so different; they happen. At most I guess I should have asked you where you wanted it, but it's part of life and living and just like a sack of crap it is good for your garden, and growing maybe, even if it is displeasing to the nose or other senses.

When I reached to grab the bird, still unsure how to go about it, it beat its wings so hard, making that buffeting sound, that it took off, its red life dripping out as it rose up, pieces that shouldn't be hanging, hanging. It was a remarkable takeoff for a pheasant, even if it had had its bottom half. The beating of its wings filled the air and it kept rising and sailing away. I followed it with my eyes, the sound growing quieter and quieter. I hoped it would never land, or that it would die in the air like some migratory birds do. But in the distance, half in the sun, several hundred metres away, I saw it clumsily make a landing in a gully, crashing into the long grass. But of course pheasants always land awkwardly like this; that is why you never see pheasants in trees—they always land with a bit of a tumble, and they like to land in the tall grass so they can crash softly into it. This would be the last crash this pheasant ever made. I stood there dumbfounded at what had just gone on, only the sound of air in my ears now, the sound of the buffeting wings still in my mind. It had all happened so quick, from the pheasant sitting there on her nest so tranquilly, time going slow, to time racing and racing as though it had gotten excited about seeing an end. I stared at the eggs, the legs, the red blood on the green grass, and then at the spot in the distant field where the pheasant lay dying or hopefully dead. I know a pheasant probably has simple thoughts, but I wondered what it thought, to suddenly go from unquestionably living to dying. I am guessing a person's thoughts aren't much more complicated than a pheasant's when they are about to die.

"So this is it?" is probably about all I would think if I was about to die—and there have been a few hairy moments in my life when I have thought that. I don't think your whole life really flashes before you or that there is some meaningful white light. I see a white light when a stick pokes me in the eye. It is probably along the lines of "so this is it, I want to live, no not yet, the earth, the world, I know people, people who will still be living after I die," and other than that there is not much I believe.

I picked up the legs, looked at them and then put them down again. I trudged toward the gully to find the pheasant. I wished Sally was back here to help me, or at the very least the comforting tick of a clock, but nothing. I couldn't even hear my feet walking along, or notice them. Once I reached the gully I looked everywhere, but I didn't find the pheasant. I started walking in grid patterns through the long grass in the gully, but still nothing. A couple times I thought I saw it, but there was nothing, sort of like Mr. Crowe after he went. I tried to convince myself that maybe I had just imagined everything, that I had been pleasantly mowing along and that there was no pheasant, no death. But the eggs and the legs put a stop to those thoughts, wouldn't let me forget. I went back to the field and kept mowing smaller and smaller rectangles of grass until nothing, thinking of pheasants and pheasant-related thoughts.

And now I sit on the couch and think some more. I have remembered death, not just of pheasants, but of everything, of my own, of all I know. I get up, walk up Cemetery Hill and go and look for the pheasant once more, wondering if it might still be crouched in the long grass somewhere, seeing the same beautiful sunset I do. But I find nothing, and on the way back I hop the fence and look at the cemetery and indulge myself in thoughts of death some more, of what it all means, so I can put a tentative check on my mental list to show I have gone over it for now, and hopefully it can let me rest for a bit, just for a while. The stone at the gate in the front says the cemetery was founded in 1789, but people died before that. They must have put them out in the fields, at the edges where the grass grows high, with the pheasants.

There are so many stones, yellow lichen on them, old rose bushes that were planted years ago and christened with tears. The place is beautiful, still, the view of the mountain and the weight of the air, but no one stays in this field on the hill long, not alive anyways; those who aren't alive stay forever. These stones are a person's final attempt at immortality, a piece of granite with your name on it. People go through life wanting to do something, achieve something: invent something that can help humanity and be the foundation for future ages, create something that will forever be appreciated, write a book or some words whose sentiments and wisdom will prove to be everlasting—some shiny static everlasting words, to make some difference, to give meaning to their hanging-around, eating, wooden-bowl-remarking, field-circling, lily-of-the-valley-smelling existence, to create a splash bigger than they are in a world where they are only a ripple, and one heading for a shore with many ripples ahead and behind them. Under these stones lie so many stories, so many dinnertime conversations, people who hung out with dogs, couples side by side, who met each other and had a story about it, who would tell it and laugh as they stole glances at each other, and who died a few months apart. They all lived like we do, thinking they'd probably never die. They knew they'd die, but not really, like we know that infinity is a possibility, but can't really fathom it—like we know there is an incredible number of stars when we look up on a clear summer night, but incredible is just a word that is easy to throw around.

It happens to a fisherman and even a fisherwoman sometimes, leaving restless houses, swamped, caught in the rigging. Some of the older fishermen have come close a few times and they know you get off to the side and you hang onto something and you make sure your legs are clear. Old memorials line the shore, sometimes an old keel, half buried in the sand, sometimes even a monument like at Black Cove, where no roads go. A foundered ship resting on the beach, where sheep, cattle and people lay dead, caked in ice, no mast, for who knows how long until found, one cold frost-covered morning. A murmur and a bit of excitement rippled through a community, but fades in vastness, started to fade when it reached people who hadn't really heard of the cove mentioned or the people involved. "Where'd you say? Who? You don't say?" There it stops.

There is a stone in Pereaux Cemetery, close to where the pheasant was, a white stone with no body underneath. Maybe he went out one morning when he knew he shouldn't, maybe for a moment close to the end he would have given anything for a note. The stone says, "Capt. J. M. Newcombe ... Lost at Sea ... Feb. 21, 1903 ... Aged 31 years." This man lived, he pondered, probably came to the same cemetery he was never buried in sometimes to see another soul who had passed, and he looked out over the fields and up at the North Mountain. I don't doubt he had a story where a pheasant scared the hell out of him as he walked through the long grass in the middle of the night, different time and place. I know he was here, but not a person alive today could ever remember his face. It's easy to forget him though; he left no eggs or legs for me to pick up and put down again, see with my own eyes. My mom worries and frets when she sees me going out with my hair in a mess, my dad worries and frets when a piece of machinery breaks, Ron worries when he finds his wheelbarrow broken, the MacInnises and I worry when we break a wheelbarrow, and sometimes it all matters, and other times you think about the stones and the stories, those numbers after names in the paper, and you wonder why people care, what makes people keep going and why they care.

Some people get tired and leave on their own terms, go out in a boat, leaving behind a paper on which a history before it happened was wrote. We had been aware of it in our area a few times. Someone like Mr. Crowe, who grew tired and finally paddled out into the Minas Basin, but only the boat ever came back—came back on the giant forty-foot tide. Maybe it was a tired day, a day where other people just looked out their window and sighed. We all looked for him. I remember distinctly Matt, Scott and I combing the beaches. Everything that we found now had to be questioned, nothing went unquestioned:

"Here's an old buoy," Scott said. "Looks like it's been there some time though."

And up in the tide line, in amongst the seaweed, clam and crab shells and old nurse shark and skate egg shells: "I found a granola bar wrapper …" Matt said.

"Do you think he would have taken a granola bar with him?" I said, thinking it wouldn't have made sense.

"I don't know," said Matt.

"I don't know either. I really don't," I said, not wanting him to take the question any other way. Scott just looked over at us without saying anything, probably figuring we had said all that needed to be said about the granola bar wrapper.

Just the winter before, I recalled, Mr. Crowe had happened by on his cross-country skis, which was unusual in itself. We had been outdoors behind the house, in the quiet gully, the one where the aerial runway had been, working on a ski jump. He gave our jump a go a few times. One time he practically landed on his head, but he earned all of our respect (what more can you ask for in life?) just for trying. Especially at his age, in his sixties, whizzing down the ramp and going over a jump that even we were all a little nervous about. We all really thought that was something, and that it took a special kind of person, and that maybe when we were older we would hopefully be the type of person to give a jump like that a try, if we just happened upon a few guys working on one out in the hills like he had.

"Remember how he tried our ski ramp last winter?" Paul said, after more fruitless searching. We were all sitting in the chairs in the kitchen, in the evening, near the door to the basement, with the old-fashioned latch.

"Yeah" and "Oh yeah," different people said at the same time.

"I can't imagine," Scott said. Then he got up to find something to eat in the kitchen, maybe to give his mind a break because I think we all were thinking how Mr. Crowe had seemed all right when he was with us going over the ski ramp, and how things had turned out, and you had to wonder what he missed, what we were missing, what someone was missing.

Like the pheasant, he was never seen again, not for sure. Some people say they saw him later, out walking along a busy street, in a crowd, never close, but I don't think so. Some people saw him everywhere, but most nowhere. Ron was given his old boots. Ron says he still wears those boots in the winter, even though they don't keep the wet out too good. And I thought that said something. I don't know what exactly. Maybe there is something there, an uncertain piece of evidence, saying something about art, sentiment, and the mostly missed intricacies of human nature. Pure practicality and efficiency could never make up a religion, at least not alone. Not when people will wear a pair of old boots even though they don't always keep the wet out.

After the day of the pheasant (and there are other days where the thing that spurs the thought is not a pheasant, but other things, more laudable things, people who didn't see the pheasant as it flew away might say) I think about these things off and on, but less and less, at least on account of the pheasant. And the passing remarks, conversations, stories and the actions they are in connection with roll on.

Weeks later I am out driving on the tractor again, after supper once more, back to clearing a field, back to clearing a space in the ridiculous. There's no thought of lists, and now I'm singing, "you really don't like it … rock the Casbah, rock the Casbah …." And I don't know what a Casbah is, and I don't care, and I don't wonder why I am not a famous singer or already half immortalized, I only assume I naturally could or will be. At the moment I am oblivious to the fact that a stranger from Pereaux, living on the Hubbard Mountain Road with a "No Exit" sign at the end, who walked out onto the stage (noise for the sake of noise on a grand scale) with hay chaff in his hair and dusty shorts on, singing half-remembered lyrics of someone else's old song only half in tune, wouldn't be as famous as I think … as he thinks he could be. But I don't think about that, same way I have no time to think about a lot of things—I don't always think about the people lost at sea, the relatives who had blood clots in their legs, the horrific car crashes, tarps laid across uncomfortable roads, the people who leave on their own terms leaving notes with voices that come from nowhere, about the Christmas tags my family has recycled for years, so that every once in a while I'll put one that reads "from Uncle Alan" on a gift even though he hasn't been with us for fifteen years, and about the pheasants out in the field.

So in fields pheasants die and pheasants are born—people too, and it's not much different whether you understand it, like it, or don't. And things move all about, the tides roll in and out, breezes blow, down the roads, over hills; people slowly amble in and out of barns, light fires in their stoves, keep their farms or drive to work; an old man feels tired and leans his thick old hand on a fence and thinks of things he has seen, thinks of loved ones and hopes dreams can be inherited and so live on. A little girl, only four, dances on an old wooden pallet while her older generations look on, trying to remember if they were ever so young and full of energy, and give silly laughs as though at something that they had almost forgotten, and they couldn't believe that they could have. A young woman with a smile and a scrunched-up nose, talking in an unnatural voice, offers her niece and nephew some sweets, to outstretched, dirty hands they say are clean. Porcupines nibble on trees; a little dog plays with a small green apple it found on the ground, but only if you watch. Deer graze, stop and stare; skunks sniff out culverts; around some tables sit mismatched chairs with mismatched people in them, words are spoken and dissipate, curious, sad, angry, glad—a million circumstances. Near me in the world Sally lies down, down by the barn, with a groaning "harumph" as she waits for me, as though I should know better but she guesses she will put up with me, and I keep driving the tractor, out in the field, for now, but soon to come back. And everything keeps on keeping on, most people happy to be alive—which is different from always being happy and probably better, because that's the biggest wonder, that we are all here, even if half the time it is only to stand around gawking at each other, hands in our pockets, not always knowing what to do with them, or what to say exactly, because there is so much not to know.

12 *The Bizarre Particulars of a Day (& a Dried-Up Frog)*

Weather-wise, I suppose most would consider it to be a beautiful day. It was fairly sunny out and there was only a slight breeze coming in off the ocean—but to me it seemed a little grey I'm afraid. There's the old saying, "You have to make hay while the sun shines." That is what I was doing. I was taking the tether down to the fields on the dike to shake out the hay that had been cut the day before. This is one of my favourite jobs because very little can go wrong with the tether and all I am required to do is drive around and around the rectangular field. I look forward to the job, because despite the RPM hours the tractor gauge will read after I am done, and despite the countless turns I make, I really go nowhere. This I find gives me plenty of time to reflect and to think, without having to worry about getting lost along the way, or missing something, and I enjoy that. When I am outwardly at my busiest and most productive, I am mindless—but when I am sitting idle and by all outside accounts unproductive, that is when my mind is flying and looking in unopened doors. I find driving around a field is the best for thinking: long stretches of sitting idly with periodic quick turns at the corners. The stretches allow me to think and the small bit of compulsory thought at the corners keeps me from growing weary and possibly falling asleep. Anyway, already I've let this line of thought carry me in one direction for too long, so here I'll give a turn.

There was no reason to think that day was going to be unlike any other day. When feeling a little low life begins to seem routine—or maybe when life is routine you feel a little low—though some people appear to embrace routine and are more content for it. But for me the more depressed I am, the more life is absorbed into this routine category. Things that would otherwise delight me no longer have that shine or lustre that they once did.

I climbed onto the old Case 1210 tractor and headed down the driveway and out the low winding dirt road with the banks on either side, towards the dike that I intended to shake out. This was a slightly longer route than going by the farm, but I enjoyed it. I sometimes do this just to see what the rest of the world is doing. I prefer living a little off the beaten trail, as they say, but every once and a while I find a need to come out of the woods, if you will, and to venture onto one of the main roads, which to me is any road that is paved. Plus, when I take this route I usually meet up with Sally, who will chase me all the way to the field. Once I get there

I always get off the tractor to say hello and talk to her for a while. Sally is no longer a pup, although I can remember when she was. She is now around seven or eight. She is a large dog but when I see her I usually go over and pick her up in my arms as though she were a little puppy; she still acts like it, the way she gets so excited. She loves to be picked up and held. She will just sit there in my arms, completely content, licking my face. If I sit down she will run over and sit in my lap, just enjoying the closeness and company of another animal on this earth. She is just as happy to see me as I am to see her. Sometimes if I get her worked up she will break into a sprint and run in tight circles as fast as she can, the thrill of using her energy up. Usually she runs in circles until she runs full speed right into my legs, and then she usually falls down herself. If Sally could laugh she would be laughing as she fell, because she looks like she wants to laugh. Some people would be quite annoyed with this, but I think it's pretty good. I don't care if I get knocked down, and I don't care if I get my clothes dirty. I am not going anywhere more important than right where I am standing, and the clothes are generally dirty anyway. They are the same clothes I wore the day before, and maybe even the day before that. Who cares if Sally knocks me down and gets me a little dirty? People worry too much about getting dirty; I worry about people who don't get dirty enough. A little dirt looks good on a pair of pants.

There are many parallels between myself and Sally, I think. When I look into Sally's brown eyes it seems as though she is just as intelligent as I am … although she is not known as being an exceptionally smart dog. I may know a few things that she doesn't, but it seems as though she has one up on me on a couple of things as well. On this particular day she seemed much happier. She must be doing something right, I thought. I wondered what it was. She never wakes up in the morning to go shake out a field—or maybe it's that she lives for every moment; I never picture her thinking too far into the future. After I got back on the tractor Sally ran around the field as happy as could be, constantly being distracted and going to investigate various things, sniffing a tuft of grass, running across the field, jumping into the creek, biting at the water—the whole place was a playground. She seemed delighted with whatever was placed in front of her. Sally lifted my spirits slightly, but now that I was back up on the tractor—she knew what that meant—I was no longer very interesting to her.

Her constant distractions and investigations soon took her out of my sight, and I was left to the reality of the task at hand. I started to circle the field. It is something I have done many times before, but this time, after a few passes something caught my eye on the ground in the short, recently-cut grass on the edge of the field. Even on a day when the shining sun is not enough to turn my mind to happier thoughts, I am not completely devoid of my own distractions and investigations. I turned off the diesel engine of the Case and jumped down for a closer look. It appeared to be a large, dried-up, mummified leopard frog that had probably been hit by either the tractor or the mower the other day when the field was cut. The scorching midday sun of the day before had dried it out. Whatever killed it had knocked the little creature's stomach out of its body so that it was hanging like a sac out of its mouth. I felt a tinge of sadness, but I soon went beyond that to a sort of philosophical curiosity. As I looked at it and wondered, I wanted to know more. So I opened up the stomach, hanging, dried, from its mouth, to see what it had eaten in the last days of its life. I found a little stick and proceeded with this operation, kneeling, chin steadied on my one knee. I emptied the stomach out onto a little patch of dirt that had been nicked by the mower blade, so that whatever was inside would not be lost in the grass. It was as though I had just emptied out a little satchel of assorted jewels onto the fertile alluvial soil of the dike. Inside the stomach I found twenty or so shiny metallic beetles. There were all sorts of different sizes and types; the kind you'd only catch a glimpse of as you walked around. They were all completely intact. I guess frogs swallow their food whole and digest it later. The beetles looked as though they could walk away, but after a little poking and prodding I decided they were pretty dead. They were all different colours, the most beautiful metallic blues, purples, greens and golds. It was something to think of the frog hopping around collecting colourful little beetles. I wondered if maybe it was more attracted to the colourful ones. The idea sort of humanized the frog to me, gave it a little personality. I smiled at the thought of the frog getting excited and chasing the particularly colourful beetles. After seeing the frog I looked up at the trees and could see each tree individually. I was deeply aware for a long moment of how alive everything was. I was seeing everything individually and not as a whole; sometimes people lose sight of the individuals. I could see individual leaves rustling on a tree, I saw other frogs, I saw other beetles, I saw the individual blades of grass. I was suddenly appreciative of the salty breeze blowing in off the ocean. I took a deep breath and was happy to be part of it all. Who knows, maybe someone right then was looking at me, or maybe someone somewhere was just looking at something and was feeling what I was feeling right then.... When you are feeling a little low, there is a definite lack of mystery. Everything is so mechanical, so predestined, so uncaring, you see sometimes dreary wholes and not individuals. I looked up and started to study the North Mountain. It was the first time I had really given it a good look that day. The dike land was overshadowed by it. Most of the frogs I'd seen would probably spend their entire lives within a couple of miles of this very field. A couple-mile radius, yet they would go about their business, hopping around the field, sometimes interacting with other little frogs, who might also have an eye for the more colourful beetles. I think that was the first time I had smiled that day.

I worked all day. I finished the field after supper and I made my way to the little access road, happy for now with my couple-mile radius, my frogs. I slowed when I approached the main road and then, with a quick turn of my head both ways I throttled up and out, the front forks making the familiar clacking as I hit the edge of the asphalt. The sound of the large wheels on the road, a few globs of mud flung high, a few pressed into the road, one arm on the fender—the paint had been rubbed off from years of the same—past the church, down the road, the air cool near the creek. I smelled the water and vegetation and thought of water skippers and trout, intricate flowers in a distant remote swamp clearing, blooming, fading, never seen. I parked the tractor, the engine off, the world quiet except for birds. My legs felt light; I walked down to the little farmhouse. You could see the fireflies going down in the swamp; once the dew set in they'd lose their fear and venture out over the lawn. Later I lay in bed, thinking, not yet tired, the peepers calling in the night.

13 *We Went, We Came Back; It's Something You Do*

The winter days were short and cold, although, with less to do than in the booming days of summer, we often felt them long enough. We were completely in the winter's depths. It was the time of year when warmer days are only a memory—a somewhat unbelievable one. The days of swimming, walking around in bare feet, no need for a shirt—or of watching a fat bumblebee as it makes its rounds to the fragile flowers, the intermittent sound of buzzing followed by short silences as it stops at each one, the pauses seeming like sounds in themselves—these were all so long ago, and so long till they would be again. Occasionally when the day was particularly grey I might find myself crunching through the snow, crossing some field or another, and then on a sudden impulse I would stop; as I looked out over the quiet landscape, the low-hanging sky, feeling the light gusts of wind—barely enough to bend a long piece of browned grass from last year poking up through the snow—I would think to myself that with my steps maybe time had stopped too. Only the breeze still had a reason to move.

People bunkered down, sometimes putting hay bales around the foundations of their houses, sometimes spruce boughs, sometimes seaweed, if they were close enough to the ocean—usually nothing though I guess; it was the houses that had something around them that you usually noticed I suppose. It was a time for closing all the doors that were able to be closed; a door on an old shed that had become incapable of closing in the middle of some rainy months, because of the sagging of the building around it, suddenly looked as though it were a whole lot more of a problem than it had in those warmer months. In the summer the door to the house was only a thin screen, one that was as easy to push aside as a cobweb, and it would clack closed by itself with the spring, always to the same little drumbeat, and in an amount of time that my mind knew precisely as I walked away. From the amount of steps you took in that faithful interval a person could gauge his mood or her urgency, sometimes making it no further than the porch, having stopped to take it all in. Sometimes you'd be halfway across the yard before the door stopped clacking, hurried by some manufactured importance. But on a usual day you'd be the same number of steps that you knew well, and from that you would understand that you were in your usual frame of mind; it was another day.

It somehow made a place seem more inviting, having the screen door—but now, in the winter, those big solid doors of oak, that for part of the year went completely unnoticed against the wall, were always closed tight. Sometimes you had to put your shoulder into them, they would stick, and sometimes you had to go through two or three sets of them before you got into the part of the house where you wanted to be. That was how I thought about winter sometimes, a time of hard sticky doors, a time when the world didn't want to make it easy for you to go anywhere. Other times though, I thought about the way the buildings were like fortresses, warm, a barrier between me and the cold, the dark of the nights, and the often dark days. Sometimes we had soft snowfalls: little wind and large, soft, floating snowflakes, which really seemed to take their time falling to earth. Flakes that had been picked up off the Bay of Fundy, you would say, and everyone knew what you were talking about. But sometimes the storms were so bad, the snow would drift so high, and the wind blow so hard that I almost thought maybe this was the end—the storm might continue to escalate, and the earth would storm itself right to death. I wondered if this was a natural storm, and I was glad I had my house with food and the fire and plenty of wood, and I hoped it was strong; I hoped it would be my little ark.

This was the Atlantic Canadian winter. A cold wet affair that you would be proud to live through. The people, the winter, the weather; they had all been there. Later if you were to talk to a person who didn't know about such things, it would be with that certain tone in your voice, a feeling in the back of your throat and a warmth in your eyes, as you thought of the strength of the family of neighbours you counted yourself part of; winter is the season that separates people in their little houses, but also brings them together.

There was going to be a bit of a gathering at the MacInnises' that winter night. Celebrating-for- celebration's-sake sort of thing. Their parents weren't going to be home and that seemed to make it the right time to bring in a few more people to fill in the void. Fill the void and then some. Plans were made, people were informed, and that night at the end of that long dead-end road, what was left of the Hubbard Mountain like a long thin peninsula stretching out into the wood and country, there was going to be a gathering. People were going to come together and feed off each other's energy, take console in knowing they weren't alone, enjoy their knowledge of each other and their bits of shared history, take comfort in their numbers, and toast and revel in the making of more history—more of the journey, more time passed.

Not a lot happens sometimes, but usually enough. There is never any fun in anything if you don't make it yourself. It all comes out of the mind. Sometimes you have to have a bit of a sense of humour about everything. Scott had bought an old snowmobile a couple weeks earlier; that was something, something like what I am talking about. Scott knew how to go about it sometimes. The thing was a monster. He had bought it for fifty bucks. Scott and I could see the potential in the thing; some were skeptical however. It was blue, the skis were short, skinny and flimsy, and the track was long, fat and thick and made out of steel in parts. It wasn't very fast; the body was made out of solid steel. The gas tank was an old red jerry can with hoses coming out of it. After you drove it your clothes and hair smelled of gasoline and mixing oil. There's a part where you have to keep your humour, not get too caught up on some of the lesser points, remember not to take yourself too seriously. The snowmobile was as old as anything, but the engine wasn't that old. The snowmobile had a 440 in it out of a newer Ski-Doo, and that Ski-Doo had been fast. The story was it had been zipping along one day and one of the skis somehow dipped below the crusty snow, caught, and it wrecked. The motor was still good though. Somehow it seemed as though the old snowmobile had taken over the newer engine, though, made it like it was, old and smelly. Old and smelly or not, we still liked it all right, and we liked it because we didn't have any other snowmobile to like. The snowmobile was heavy and unfortunately was no friend to the environment; the blue-grey smoke would pour out of it as you went. Even though the engine used to make the former, newer, more lightweight Ski-Doo go pretty fast, this old snowmobile still drove like an old, tippy three-wheeled tractor. We were always having to work on it, too, taking it apart to recoil the pull-cord, making sure it was getting spark, getting fuel, that sort of thing. I remember we showed the old thing to a couple of girls who had come down to Nova Scotia on an exchange from the territories (the alternate to Paul's trip) and they had wondered what the thing was. They didn't want to go near it, and they didn't like the way we smelled after we had been around it. This didn't bother us though. We always liked a good laugh at our own expense.

To give you a little taste of the spirit of the snowmobile, a few days earlier, before the party, we had all been enjoying the heat of the kitchen and the laziness of having nothing to do. We were watching Scott out the window, without much real interest, as he was doing something or other to the machine. Gearing it up for a great snowmobile race, we may have joked. He yanked on the pull-cord and somehow or other the throttle was stuck wide open, from the humidity and cold, and off the snowmobile went without anyone on it. Out over the field, like an animal let free—it raced across the openness towards the distant trees, roaring triumphantly. You could almost have rooted for it. It seemed to be going fast enough then, it jumped and bounced as it hit the drifts. Scott was right behind in pursuit, kicking up the snow like his throttle was stuck wide open too; it was good to see the energy in Scott, made you smile. Finally the old snowmobile hit a drift and flipped over. That got us all going pretty good, when we saw that. We all looked at each other and laughed, some almost buckled over. It wouldn't take much to get us all going when we were looking for a thing to laugh at.

I remember it was a really cold and windy day too, had a nor'easter. Earlier I had been walking along, across the frozen ground and snow, and I had looked up and seen a crow futilely fighting it out with the cold wind above my head. It struggled and struggled, glided in the wind, losing ground for a moment, moving laterally, back and forth as it tried to balance on the current. It struggled again, with a few beats of its wings, and then, in a snap, gave up, swung around, and with surprising speed but no real effort glided seventy yards or so and perched high in a tree in the nearby forest. There it sat and I wondered what it thought now. Content? Mad at the wind? I wondered what I would think. I had stopped to watch, but after it landed I turned to go. I have seen that same thing happen a number of times—usually I don't remember until I see it happen again—a bird unable to get through the wind like that, maybe not always a bird. Whenever I see a crow or a bird struggling like that it strikes a chord like I have seen the same thing a million times, even if I can't recall exactly where or when. For some reason on that day, while we were laughing at Scott and his antics (and Scott would have been laughing too had he been standing there with us), I recalled that crow, and the thought of it sobered me up a little.

After the excitement, everyone decided to go about something or other, and I went and put a jacket on and strolled outside to see if I could lend Scott a hand. He would need help to right the heavy old thing. He was smiling as I walked over to him. Scott knew you had to roll with things like that—no sense tiring yourself out getting too caught up in it.

The party was beginning to get underway. People arrived and the music was turned up loud. The MacInnises and myself were loitering around as people rolled in. Familiar names and familiar faces poured through the door: Jer, Eben, Dale, Kelly, Jen,

 Danielle … the Butlers, the Reagans. Drinks were made up. Strange drinks, drinks that had no names, drinks that were given names just minutes before and then passed around. "Give me another one of those … whatever it is you called it … you know …." People laughed and people hugged. People always asked how you were doin' when they first saw you, people always wanted to know how you were doin', maybe so they could tell how they were doin'.

I'd be lying if I said I could tell you exactly what it was; I am not sure what went on. Sometimes a person isn't ready for a party maybe, doesn't understand the reason. Sometimes you are unsure, your mind is elsewhere, it distracts you with thought, the thinking gets in the way. Maybe it isn't all going the way you like—there've been too many of those grey days in a row, or perhaps you yourself are struggling, futilely fighting against something, if only in your mind. If only you had a tree in which to catch your bearings, wait it out, figure it out.… It's harder to do that in your mind, I think.

I had started to drink a beer, a Keith's, only one, and already people were way ahead of me—they were ahead of me before they came. I walked around, I smiled, I did not say a whole lot. I thought, but I did not say a whole lot. Other people said lots with little thought, not bad though, it is the sort of thing one has to do. I can't say I am sure of anything sometimes.

I could tell Scott was thinking, and let me not pretend too much to have known what he was thinking, but he was thinking. Something was going on in his head, and even though he was just walking around sort of slow and not moving in one direction or another too quick, I think he was restless. It was sort of like he would turn quick like he knew he wanted to, but when he started walking he wasn't so sure and he didn't walk as fast as he had turned. I guess really that's just how I felt. I don't know how Scott felt, but that was how I felt. Perhaps I should only say I felt like that, and let Scott answer for himself.

After a while I didn't see Scott anymore. I heard a couple people remark on it, but the music was too fast and the atmosphere too festive for it to disrupt anyone for too long. I walked out onto the porch and the cold air hit me and it made me wonder why I was there. The light radiating out from the windows seemed to be eaten up by the night outside. The dull music heard through the insulated walls of the house and the many thick doors seemed to run up against the quiet stillness of the expansive rolling countryside and the night, right there on the porch. I was standing on the verge. I stood there for a minute with my hands in my pockets; I could smell the smoke of the burning pinewood from the stove inside drifting down from the chimney; you could really smell it in the crisp air; it smelled good. I let out a breath. The light picked up on the ghost of it and used the black night as a backdrop. I blew out a few more breaths until it was no longer the same. I stared out and there was Scott, out in the yard in the dark. He was standing near his big old ugly snowmobile, his hands in his pockets, looking down at it. It was not windy anymore outside, just cold and really still, like you could hear the snow.

The dark reminded me of an ocean, you could see

 for a bit, but then things got murky and distorted; it stretched across the earth and almost infinitely into the sky. You knew there was lots out there you could not see—almost everything, actually. I stepped down off the porch.

"What are you doin'?" I asked Scott, out of habit. I guess I should have asked, "What are you thinking?" because he wasn't doing much—but "What are you doin'?" is one of those all-inclusive questions. You can get all different types of answers with a "What are you doin'?" Just standing there living and breathing is doing *something* really. It's funny how often you will get the answer "Nothin'"—or how often I give that answer. Just a reflex I suppose.

"Nothin' really," Scott said, putting off the question, guarding his thoughts.

"Everyone seems to be having a pretty good time inside."

"Oh yeah," he said genuinely, with a bit of energy. "Do you want to take her for a rip?" He gave a nod towards the snowmobile.

"Sure ... I guess." I wondered what everyone else would think. Taking off was pretty well the opposite of a party.

"Where do you want to go?" Scott said.

"It doesn't matter none."

"We could try heading her up the old Hubbard Mountain Road."

"Yeah, seems as good a place as any..." I said, just thinking about passing the time myself.

I walked back into the house and grabbed some gloves without telling anyone why. I couldn't have answered. We had no real reason to go up the mountain, there was no immediate need, nothing waiting for us up there … although I guess if you think about it too much, if given too much time to ponder about yourself, there is not much need for anyone to go anywhere, in the scheme of things, and yet the world is full of people travelling around looking for answers, without much inclination, wandering around like vagabonds, too restless to stay still, fearing the stillness. I came back out and got onto the snowmobile and we took off.

We went down into the gully behind the house and further on along a path that was on a side hill, not real fast, but fast enough; it ran pretty good. We got up some speed and made it across the creek, the thin ice cracking and flooding with water behind us. We went along a smaller field and then up through a steep narrow path through some woods to another field—then we went up the side of one of my family's apple orchards, up towards the corner where we knew there was an opening into the thick woods that was the abandoned part of the old Hubbard Mountain Road. Finally there it was, just a darker opening into the woods, blacker on black, if you can imagine. Without hesitating we went right in; the little yellow light of the snowmobile suddenly seemed brighter, contrasting with the increased darkness of the shaded forest, the thick pines. At the beginning of the road (really a path at this point) the banks were steep on either side, and the trail took a nice rounded turn to the right. The evenness of the turn told you this trail had been given some thought at one point. After that it went straight for a while and then, instead of being sheltered by banks, we were on a sort of land bridge with deep gullies on either side—still in the shade of the pines though. You could tell how parts of the road had been carved out and other parts had been built up by the hands of men many years ago. The road was very old, and no longer used, but this was the original mountain road. Parts of it were far steeper than you would find on any road meant for the cars of today; maybe that was why it was abandoned. I thought about what it must have been like to go up with a horse and carriage—or maybe, many many years ago, there were people who made similar midnight runs up the old wooded road in the winter, but on horseback. People don't always tell things like that, they often don't say much about a lot of things like that or about what is on their mind. When they talk they rarely scratch the surface of their mind; they've trained themselves not to. Who knows what kind of history an old road like this might have? I bet some of the most interesting stories have long since been forgotten—things that are never told because a person is afraid no one will listen and no one will care. There are so many stories. Lives were lived, people born, people died; doctors, pastors, homesteaders and, most interestingly, regular people like me would have made this climb, and this road was part of it all. I could relate to some of those stories I'm sure.

I know I had heard that there was a pastor who preached in several churches, and every week he would make the trek by horse-drawn carriage over the mountain to spread the word to some of the other little churches that dotted the countryside. On each leg of the journey he got a ride from some farmer or other soul who thought it a worthy cause. Little churches and farms carved out of the woods here and there all over the countryside, connected by these little roads through woods so thick that the trees came together overhead, the roads always in the shade, even in late summer, with the sun right overhead.

We rode along, sometimes slower, sometimes faster, looking at things as we went. Some of the time I was almost blind with my eyes open, thinking inside myself, while other times I let what my eyes saw more or less govern my thoughts—wondering at things, sometimes thinking I saw something in the dark. Sometimes it may have been something, other times probably nothing at all, not always sure which was the case. Riding along on the snowmobile like this was a lot like life in general: going along, not always sure what you were seeing, not always sure just why, content to be moving along though.

When I looked into the dark abysses that were gullies, or when the snowmobile's yellow light showed a big old rock right near the trail, maybe too big for a team of oxen to move, it gave me a weird sense. When I saw these things my thoughts were focused on the outside, but the sight of them would produce thoughts that brought me inside so for a while I became almost blind again. Like the rock, the woods were so lonely at this time of night, people did not use this part of the Hubbard Mountain Road much. It was weird to think that my eyes were not the first to look at this particular rock—a little hat of snow on the top with a bit of green moss still clinging to the side even in winter. Maybe those scratches on its side were a hundred years old, left behind from where chains had futilely been attached. Maybe I was not the first to wonder at it. Years before, many people used the road; Native people too, their landscape carved by Glooscap and other legends that were written down and passed along by the Delhaven Rands' ancestor Silas. That was before the road was even thought of, maybe it was only a deer path. It seemed like a rock like that or a gully might say so much if it could—but they just sat there and you could only wonder what their stories were, what their take on the world was. It's the same sort of feeling you might get looking into the soft smiling eyes of a young child in an old black-and-white photograph, and then being told it's your grandmother or grandfather, or great-grandmother or great-grandfather, who passed on years before. Suddenly those eyes don't seem like a laughing child's at all; they look as though they are just the cover on something, on a thousand answers, answers to the questions in your head. You wonder about those eyes, become transfixed by them, mesmerized, staring into them as they seem to stare into you, searching. And you wonder about all they could tell you if they could talk, and you think about this relative and all that they had lived and felt, and you wonder where they are now, and where their memories are, if anywhere, and how all that you now think of when you look at those eyes could ever have belonged to that laughing child. You just get a sense that maybe the picture knows something, or maybe you simply will it to—you hope *someone* knows.

Twisting and turning, the wooden walls guiding us along like water through a culvert, we continued up the abandoned old road; the woods seemed deep and dark, as though they were something you could fall into. The sound of the old snowmobile jumped into the dark but was eaten up; you could tell how quiet the woods were even over the snowmobile. I wished we were quieter; it seemed dangerous to attract too much attention. The woods and the darkness made me feel small and I liked it; in the world there is some safety in being small. Like a mouse. A mouse knows dangers, but being little can be good too. A mouse will scamper away into a little hole before you even see it. You'll walk by on a path without giving it a thought; to you the mouse never was. The mouse *is* though, just not to your eyes. After you leave, out it comes again, and it can pretend again that the world is its own.

For its part the snowmobile climbed right up the trail without much trouble. It did get stuck once or twice, but not too badly. Scott and I would get off and try and lift up on the track. One of us would stand on the side and give it some gas; if it started to move we just jumped on and gunned it. It was up to us both to jump on while it was moving. You felt as though the darkness of the woods might close in around you if you were left behind. Sometimes as you ran to catch the snowmobile you'd have an urge to look over your shoulder, possibly hoping you weren't being seen or chased. Maybe people just like to assume they are always being looked at by something out there or above, be it good or bad—but not forgotten.

Finally we pulled out of the tunnel, up at the top

 of the North Mountain, into an opening. We had reached the very top—neither of us had been sure if we would. We kept going and met the newer asphalt road that went up and along the crest of the mountain. We cut the engine and got off without really saying anything. It was quiet and still—the stillness only known to a dark, winter, windless night. There were no cars on the road, most people were asleep, it was midnight. The thought of sleep is strange—as though when you close your eyes the world stops and only starts again the moment you open your eyes. You could be convinced the world waited the whole night through. Even though we were awake, standing up there at the top of the mountain, looking out over the valley, seeing the occasional porch light on here and there, it seemed like the world might have stopped for us too. I wondered how things were going down at the party; the quiet stillness made it seem a world away—the warm house with the music, the drinks and the woodsmoke so far away through the cold air, the vast dark woods separating us on the mountain from it. It's probably the same sort of infinite far-away feeling someone might get if he was out on an island by himself, looking out over the water at the mainland, but unable to swim. Scott and I lay down on the yellow line and stared up into the sky. It was a clear night and there were so many stars, they seemed so bright and numerous. I can't remember if we talked about them or not. But that doesn't really matter—they'd only have been words and they wouldn't have allowed us to understand each other any better than we already did in our own thoughts, as we each looked up at those same stars. I remember thinking that there was absolutely nothing between us and the stars. Between us and the party there was the mountain, the forest, the darkness—but there was only space separating us from the stars. Sometimes we look at things so much we're blind to them.

I have no idea how long we stayed, but I know in time we came back—that's all we really went for. We started back into the woods, slipped into them like you would into a dark, still pond, going as quietly and as stealthily as we could, not wishing to stir things up or disturb a thing. Down the mountain we travelled effortlessly, coasting along at an easy, surprising speed. The house down in the valley, where the party was, where the heat, the light, and the laughing and the people were—we headed for it like a distant shore.

We came out of the woods and down into a field. There was the house up on the hill at the end of the road that reached out like a peninsula. The house was all lit up like a lighthouse, telling us where it was in the darkness, guiding us in. The snowmobile groaned up the hill and we parked it in front of the house, close to where it had been parked before. After all the time we had been gone the party had quieted. A little stiff, we got off the snowmobile, and with nothing but a couple of mutterings about arriving, we went through the heavy door into the house, through the mud room and through another thick door. The warmth from the people and stove, and a number of curious faces, were quick to greet us.

"How are you guys doin'?" I found myself asking, just trying to act natural, trying to slip unnoticed into the atmosphere of the room, trying to duck under the thin cover of my words. My question for the most part was ignored, probably because it was seen for what it was, and in reply I got another question.

"Where were you guys?"

"We went up the mountain ..." Scott and I both found ourselves answering a couple of times as various people arrived from various corners.

"What for?" they said, but for this I couldn't really think of an answer, and all I could really do was stare for a bit, eventually saying something like "I guess ... I guess I'm not too sure ...." And yet, even when we answered like this, no one was put off, there would still be excitement in the eyes of whoever it was that asked, unsure what to make of it, of any of it, the whole thing.

"That's something," they would say, "that you did that. We didn't know where you went. I can't believe you guys just went up the mountain like that ...." It was a strange thing. We went, we came back; it's something you do. I don't know. The whole world is strange if thought about too much—doing anything is strange if thought about too much. We had not brought anything back, not even a story—not much of one anyways—and then here we were again. Changed or not changed, how the hell can you tell? Our inability to provide a reason caused the greatest interest. People visibly stopped and pondered this, but with no success, and maybe this made people think someone was finally onto something. The looks in the eyes of some of the people who asked, the smile they had when they heard we had just gone up the mountain for no reason. I think they wished they knew why we went, wished we knew why we went. Some maybe wished they had gone, broken away and gone too—gone and come back just to say they did, for no reason. People are always moving around just looking for histories, looking to make them, looking to share them. Histories seem real, something that stretches back; they are like a religion; they can answer questions.

I relaxed a little, and for a while I thought I would allow myself not to think, at least not as much, because I had already done that for a while. I had a bit of a drink, but not much. It seemed like an effort and I was enjoying my current state. In time I knew I would feel the need to move about again, to move away from something, to move towards something—to or from what I hope is not always important. We all sat around on the couch and chairs, the ones in the kitchen from the train, near the basement door with the latch. I sat contentedly; I didn't feel like moving, like a crow in a tree. I sat there in my chair and soaked in the atmosphere like the room was a warm bath. The house seemed to grow warmer, the outdoors colder; the music was now slow, soft and nice, the light from the stove dim, the people tired and weary, but still we sat and talked, only eyes and mouths slowly moving. The log that had just been placed in the stove sparked and popped, and, looking at the faces around me, I felt as though I was not alone, as though my thoughts and wonders were the same as those of the others. I didn't think I'd want to move from my chair for a while. I think it was Kelly—although the others seconded the thought with their silent eyes—who, after a time, paused in conversation, and again, remarked quietly, "I can't believe you guys just decided to take that old snowmobile up the mountain …." She said it as though to nobody, said with more thought and contemplation than let on, said with excitement, a little fear, and a smile.

14 *On Thin Ice with the Moped*

It was early spring and there was still some snow on the ground. The days fluctuated back and forth; you never knew if it was going to be warm or cold. Sometimes we'd get a little snow, but it would be packy and when you'd walk through, it would stick, turning your boots to elf shoes. One day it could be as low as minus ten and the water in the puddles would freeze—and the next day it could be as high as plus ten and the water in the puddles would thaw again and the melted snow water would come flowing down the mountain. The creek would swell to the extent that you would no longer feel comfortable calling it a creek, but instead would feel it was more properly referred to as a river. And most people held a little pride when they said they were familiar with a river, as though some of the river's greatness could be found in them just for knowing it.

The night before, we had received a new dusting of snow that covered everything, but it was destined to be gone by that afternoon for the most part. I was walking up the MacInnises' driveway and noticed next to it in a drift some things written in yellow, the meaning of which colour I shall leave to your imagination. First there were bold letters, too bold. "M… A…" and then a bit of a straight line that I guessed was intended to be a "T" but had petered out; next to it in thinner letters I saw "S… C… O… T… T…," and then extending from the top of the last "T" there were several loops and spirals—and the name was even underlined a couple of times, showing much artfulness, control and practice. I picked up my pace, wanting to see what Matt and Scott and everybody were about.

Not too far away from the MacInnises' house, a couple of gullies away, a huge irrigation pond had been built. It had been put in a few years earlier. We had excavated some old cow bones from this particular gully a while back. This gully had provided a safer site for cow-bone investigations than the field across the way, as the fences here were in disrepair and so no cows were being kept in these pastures anymore. You could not even tell where the cow skeleton had been anymore. The three soft pines that the bones had lain under were now gone. I remember when the pond was to be put in; we all had mixed feelings about it. We were not sure if we wanted the beautiful gully destroyed, but at the same time there were many advantages to having a large pond so close. Regardless, the decision was not hinging upon the opinions of a few boys. The project went ahead, and the massive pond started to take shape. As in all gullies, there was a little stream running down the middle of it, and this was to feed the pond. With bulldozers and earthmovers the pond was shaped, and the dirt was moved to the far end to form a dam which stretched from ridge to ridge. They installed some large concrete pipes and an overflow. They worked on it for weeks. The workers saw us watching them from the bushes sometimes and warned us not to go near the pond for a long time, because with a dam made out of sand like this one was you could never be sure if the dirt was settled, and it was possible the whole thing could give way. The pond was finally finished, but after all the people and equipment had gone away it took several more weeks for the pond to fill from the little stream. Eventually the water stretched way back and filled the entire gully. By most people's standards it was a lake and not a pond, because it was huge. It took up several acres. We stayed away from it for a few days, but even their warnings could not keep us from it for long. After a while the pond became one of our favourite places to go.

It had been a few years since the pond had been put in now, and we had just enjoyed a long winter with the pond, playing ice hockey, practising for the Olympics, and just doing whatever else we could think to do with the thing. The previous week we'd had a few of those plus-ten days all in a row. It happened like that: the further into spring you got the more warm days you got in a row, until they all became warm days. The ice on the pond had been thick over the winter, probably around eight inches to a foot. When we had these warm days the ice began to melt. The ice on a pond does not melt uniformly; it starts from the edges. I imagine the sun probably heats the land faster, and then the land in turn melts the ice. Over the warm spell, the thirty or forty feet closest to the bank melted, causing a large moat around the thick ice floating out in the middle. It was something to see the ice floating out there almost like a large island. It was also something how this slab of ice was so big that it did not move. It is known that ice sitting free on top of water can move pretty easily, but this ice was so huge that it would have taken a lot of energy to move it. The ice did move actually, just moved very slowly. Over several days, probably because of the wind, and maybe because of the action of the little stream, the several-acre piece of ice moved—maybe a couple of inches every day—towards the southern end of the pond. This meant that down on the southern side, where the dam and overflow were, the moat around the ice was not as wide, maybe only about twenty feet. We had ways of getting out on the ice when it was like this, and we would travel out to the ice island and run around on it. Somehow the fact that there was no easy way off the thing made it that much more thrilling.

Now I walked in the door and commended Scott for his artwork down the driveway; I think he was genuinely glad I noticed. There was more than quorum for doing something interesting that day. Paul, Scott and I were in the kitchen. Matt was in his room. Jer had just called and said he was walking over.

"I'll go get Matt," I said.

We were now having a cold snap, and the temperature had dipped down well below zero the previous night. Once Matt emerged from his bedroom, we went down to see what effect this had had on the pond. We discovered that the moat was now frozen, about half an inch thick, locking the island in place. After Jer arrived we went down to the thin ice around the edge and found that it would not support us. As soon as you ventured out you would hear cracking noises all around you and the ice would start to give. A few of us tried running over it to see whether, if you went fast enough, you could keep ahead of the breaking ice, but a few of us also got wet. You could keep ahead of the breaking ice for a few steps, but eventually you would break through. Then we had an idea.

The other day Scott and I had been working on the moped. The vehicle had been sitting in the barn for the whole winter; no one was sure if it would ever run again after the accident. Scott and I thought maybe the only thing the moped needed was the replacement of a few hoses and little things that had burnt up in the fire. We got some plastic tubing from the local hardware store and used those for the fuel lines. I think a cable had to be replaced, and after that we figured she was ready to go. We tried to start it and, about a can of WD-40 later, we had the little engine puttering along quite nicely.

We thought it would really be something if we could get the moped onto the big island of ice out in the pond. Scott, Paul, Matt, Jer and I all went back to get the moped, and then we all walked back to the pond in a big group, pushing the moped along and talking about how we would get it out there, who would ride it first and so on. We took it down to the southern end of the pond where the distance to the ice was not so great. We found a large rotten log and some boards and formed a bridge, stretching from the land to the thick ice. After a great deal of work we proudly pushed the moped onto the solid ice in the middle. We all just stood there a second, looking out over the large flat area that was to be our playground. After pausing a moment, to admire the beauty of the idea and to mentally thank God for the good time we were about to receive, we started taking turns riding about the ice on the moped.

The ice was rough with snow frozen to it in parts; in other parts puddles of water had formed and frozen again, and the ice was quite slick. It was great fun tearing around the ice on the moped, going from the rough to the slippery parts. The back tire would spin out and occasionally someone would go down. For the most part the guy on the moped would try and hit everyone else and everyone else would run around dodging and throwing snowballs at the guy riding the moped. This old game proved to be as good on the ice as in a field. We amused ourselves this way for a couple of hours. Sometimes when a few of us had grown tired of the game we would try our hand at walking out on the thin ice around the edge again. That was pretty fun too. Of course the ice was still not able to hold us, and although you might be able to make it a ways you could not make it back to shore—not dry anyways.

The fun of having the moped out on the ice was winding down and we started having notions of heading back home. It had been quite the lengthy ordeal getting the bike safely onto the ice in the first place, and we knew it was going to be an ordeal to get it back off. No one was looking forward to the work ahead, especially since, after our labours there would be no promise of hours of fun and excitement on the other side. Paul was on the moped at the time and he said he had an idea of how to get the bike off without going down to the other end of the pond and trying to ferry it across. We all knew what he was scheming by the look on his face. Paul wasn't sure if he was going to do it, and none of us were sure if we wanted to do it. We were all just standing around with half smiles on our faces, contemplating. I think any of us would have done it with a little prompting. On the one hand, we were half drunk with the idea of flying across the thin ice on the little moped, and on the other hand, we all realized—some of us to higher degrees than others—that the chances of making it across the thin ice unscathed were slim. We stood there quietly for a bit, looking at each other to see if any one of us wanted to do it more than another. Eventually I said, "Well … I'll do it if no one else is going to.…" This wasn't exactly the same as saying I would do it. I knew that my saying this would heat things up and maybe speed up the debate a little. Everyone now knew that this thing was going to get done. Knowing it was going to get done sort of upped the attraction of being the one to do it. After all, there would be much glory on the other side for the person who made it. If you were to make it, the story of flying over the thin ice on the moped would be told for ages. The idea of being that hero was a nice one. Of course there was another possibility. If the moped broke through as soon as the front tire hit the ice, then this story would go down through the ages, and you would be known as not being one of the sharpest tools in the shed, the one who got swindled into the thing, and who hadn't known any better. If the bike went through the ice, the story would be told like it had been obvious the ice could not support anyone. Anyway, I had said I was going to do it if no one else was, so at least we all knew there was going to be some story going down through the ages.

We were still standing around and a few people were still humming and hawing over whether or not they wanted to say they would do it with any conviction. Finally, in a loud voice, and in a way that suggested he did not want us to give him any more time to consider what he was doing, Paul said, "I'll do it." He was quite sure he was going to do it. I could tell he was clearing his head of any rational thoughts. That is what you had to do for this kind of stunt. I can't really say I was surprised that it was Paul. Sometimes Paul was known to chicken out on such things. I remember the long wait we all had when he was trying to jump out of the tree on the aerial runway. On the other hand, there were days when Paul had a crazy side and I would not doubt that there was nothing he would not do, the crazier the better. He would wrestle a bear, jump out of a plane, or maybe even eat the pancakes Scott made that time—the ones we later used like discuses. He'd surprise me even after I thought I had seen it all. Most of us in the group were like that. We all had our timid days, and we all had our daring days. There really was no go-to guy when a stunt was proposed. It could be any given guy on any given day. We all were pretty daring when it came down to it, if daring is the word you want to use there. Other words have been tossed around.

There was no arguing after Paul said that he would do it and we all relented rather quickly. We had taken this thing to the next step. Things had to move quickly now. We did not want to give Paul any time to consider what he was doing. We knew that time to think was a bad thing when it came to a stunt like this. We decided that Paul would cross the thin ice up at the north end of the pond. The north end was where the water from the creek flowed in and so the pond was the shallowest up there. The water might have been seven or eight feet deep right at the edge of the island. This would be good in the event that we had to fish the moped out. But the distance to the shore was also much greater up there than at the southern end. Paul would have to travel at least forty feet before he got to the shore. With a little investigation by the experts, a good site was quickly chosen, and Paul lined up at the edge of our ice island eyeing the perilously thin stretch he was about to embark out onto. He revved the little engine a couple times, maybe to try and scramble any doubting thoughts that were trying to creep into his mind. Scott, Matt, Jer and I stood around the spot he was aiming to take off from. Paul turned the moped around and drove back from the site about a hundred metres, to give himself a good runoff and some speed to hit the moat with. He lined himself up and again revved the engine a few times. There was a pause, and we all just stared at him in the distance as he sat there idling. Then, with a burst of energy and with a sudden wave of an arm like he was charging a fellow knight,

 Paul was off. It was hard to get up really good speed on the ice, but Paul probably got the little moped going around forty kilometres an hour or so. The engine was wide open. Its whine was deadened a little by the snow and ice. It was almost comical to see Paul hunched over the moped like he was going at a great speed. He had an extremely determined look upon his face. His eyes were locked on the spot he was aiming for, but the corners of his mouth hinted at a smile. Most of us thought there was a good chance that Paul would call off his charge before he even got to where we stood—some maybe even thought that might be a good idea. Not just because this whole thing might be dangerous for Paul, but because we had the moped to think about. Paul didn't let up though—he kept on coming. About ten metres from the edge he forewent his hunched position to raise his body off the bike a little. The nearer he got to us the wider his eyes became, fully trying to take in everything they could. It looked like they wanted no part in what the rest of his body was doing.

He finally reached us, and shot out onto the thin ice. We were impressed. At this point time seemed to slow. Paul was going the same speed, but now we took in every detail of what was happening. The world could have been on fire and we would not have noticed. Our eyes were all locked on Paul on the little moped crossing thin ice. Paul had made it about twenty feet, nearly halfway, and the stunt was already a complete success. For a split second we all wished it was us out there on the moped. For a moment anything seemed possible—the sky was the limit. We now knew the rules of the world really didn't apply to us, just as we had suspected. Paul continued on his course. It really seemed like he was going to make it the whole way across. He had travelled about thirty feet when it happened. First his back tire dropped down through the ice, slowing him down, and then the whole thing, Paul and all, crashed through. The bike vanished. The engine sounded for a few seconds under water through the bubbles and then stopped. Paul crashed his way, half swimming half running, through the last ten feet, to emerge on the shore thoroughly soaked from the waist down.

Paul had crashed through the ice, but he had not lost. Really the whole thing could not have gone any better, when we thought about it. Paul had almost made it, which was amazing, plus we had gotten the excitement of seeing him break through the ice. Finally, the moped was only a little ways off the shore, so it would be easy to retrieve.

The rest of us quickly made our way down to the southern end of the pond, to cross onto the shore and congratulate Paul and ask him how he had felt flying across that thin ice. We ran around and found him just standing there grinning. He said that he had thought he was going to make it when he was around the middle. He had cut up his legs pretty good when he went through the ice. It had dug into him when he went crashing through. That was something that none of us had considered, but now we knew; that was interesting. Since no one else looked like they were going to, Scott and I took it upon ourselves to fish the moped out of the water. We waded in and managed to lug the thing out, getting our clothes thoroughly soaked in the process—but we couldn't just leave it there. The water was freezing, and the mud felt weird on our boots in the cold water—something about feeling that mud when there was still snow and ice around. We pulled the moped up on shore, and there was mud and seaweed stuck to the handlebars. But it was good to see her out of the water again. Knowing the resilience of the moped, I half expected it to start right up again after we got it out, but it didn't. There was probably some water in the carburetor. It had probably made its way in through the air intake. It would take some work to get her going again. Walking back towards the house, pushing the moped up the hill, we noticed that the little streamlined silver lamp on the front of the bike was half filled with water and this made us laugh. When we got back to the house we put the huge pot on the stove element so we could boil up a heap of spaghetti. We warmed ourselves and dried our clothes around the wood stove, and even though we'd all been there, we started to tell the story of the moped—bits and pieces of the story being told by different people—and we laughed.

15 *Feels Like You're Doin' Somethin'*

Early morning is the natural habitat of the idea. Occasionally it may wander into other parts of the day, but this is more rare. With an idea, all other things having stayed the same, a day can go from dull to exciting. This was one of those ideas that built up over the course of a conversation, attracting energy from all involved: people said their little bits here and there, all four of us had a part, the words pieced themselves together into something—an idea. "What are you doing … nothing … yeah … sunny out … mmmhmm … you have any breakfast? … eggs … who left the shovel out on the lawn? … I don't know … someone better move it before someone sees … yeah … any eggs left? … I saw some in the barn … what should we do today? … I don't know … someone better move the shovel … I like digging with a shovel sometimes … yeah, feels like your doin' somethin' … there any other shovels around do you know? ...." And so there it was. Ideas: they just spring up sometimes on their own pretty well; like raising a spoonful of letters out of alphabet soup and discovering you have spelled a word. You know you've had a hand in it, maybe you even show it around a bit; still, your part was simply recognizing it. You know deep down you can't really take too much credit, not without feeling a little guilty.

As we sat there in the kitchen—getting breakfast, worrying about shovels, waking up—not too far away, across some grassy gullies, there was a perfect place to dig a hole or maybe form a subterranean dwelling of some sort. The ground was soft and rolling and the grass was thick but never came above the knee. There was the odd wild apple tree—they had apples that would get ripe, but never very red—planted there by animals or birds. In places the pine forest took over, but in other places the grass seemed to win out. It was an interesting mosaic. At the bottom of one of the gullies there was an old seeder, left there probably fifty years ago or more by some farmer, and an old Model A Ford, both sunk deep into the ground, half gone like old memories; these were the only signs of humankind. I can remember the first time I saw them. I had been wading up the creek and I came out of the swamp and there in the gully was the old car, quite unexpected, like coming upon a stranger in the middle of the woods just standing completely still and not saying anything and being a little shocked, wondering what his story is or why he's there. The MacInnis boys already knew about the Model A; it was something they knew so well that they forgot to tell me about it. It would be like telling somebody they had an ass—you just would figure they already knew.

I liked finding the old car there. It was something from the past and something that wouldn't regenerate, unlike the giant raised-up anthills that were constantly being worn down and built up at the same time, or the alders in the swamp that were always growing and dying, a dead branch falling down on this side, a new shoot sprouting up on that side, forever old and young. I tried to imagine the trees around the Model A a little shorter, and the car with all four tires sitting on top of the ground and not sunk in, as though it had just been parked there. It is somehow a lot different to find an old sunken car like that than it would be to find a newer one sunk into the ground somewhere. You paint a little time and history on a thing and almost anything is beautiful in a mysterious sort of way. Maybe this only goes to expose the human uncertainty of knowing where we came from, or why we're here. We like seeing a little history on a thing, a little certainty.

Roland Porter had used to live in the MacInnises' big old farmhouse; he was born and raised there. Back then there were a couple large barns and some outbuildings, but now there were only a few dips and rocks in the lawn that you would occasionally catch a mower on, and a mysterious rock wall out in the field. Roland was in his late eighties now. We had only ever met him a few times. He now lived in Ontario, but he was the type of person you only had to meet a couple of times and you would think you'd known him longer. He only had three strong fingers on each hand when he was born, same as his father and going back I'm not sure how long. It ran in the family and I guess his father held that against him. Back then it was commonly thought that something wrong on the outside meant something wrong on the inside—same way that when my father was just a boy his teacher always tried to make him write with his right hand even though he was left-handed. To write with his left hand was something different, not the norm, the mark of the devil. I remember shaking hands with Roland and his grip was as strong as any I had ever come across; the three good fingers were larger than normal and powerful. One time Scott got spooked in the old farmhouse when he thought he was by himself and he saw a shadow that was not his own with three large muscular fingers resting at its side. Roland had promised he would come back to haunt the house if it ever came to that.

On his occasional visits back to the Valley he would look around the land he had lived on in his younger years. He could look at parts and remember when wide open field used to be forest and when forest used to be wide open field. He could point to trees that he was a father to, whom he had known when they weren't even knee-high, but whom had now outgrown him, like sometimes happens, and had turned into strong, sturdy wards of this earth. Histories are all about perspective, no matter who is telling them, and Roland's historical perspective was an interesting one. I remember him saying that the old Model A used to be his—it had been his first car. A single-seater with a rumble seat in the back. He'd bought it for fifty bucks and fixed it up himself. He once wrote me about the car and said, "To someone so poor as I it was part of the dreaming process." When Scott and I had been out in the yard working on an old Camry or a Corona, or the Dodge Colt (which when anybody asked we would remind was imported from Mitsubishi), thinking about trips and freedom, I had never really pictured us as dreamers, but then I guess I had never really tried to picture us. When you are young you always assume that you are the first to do or think everything that you do or think—that things are different this time around.

After breakfast we procured a couple more shovels and a pickaxe and, like four dogs, Paul, Scott, Matt and I started out across the hills, running, dodging around and leaping over the grassy anthills, dragging the shovels by their handles, the metal blades bouncing along behind us. Every once in a while we'd use them like short vaulting poles. We were each trying to anticipate our direction, occasionally glancing back, like a dog will do, and trying to outpace one another, alternating between chasing and being chased. It was never really clear which was which or who was following whom, or even where we were going, but we got there. Whether we were just tired or something called us right to the spot, we got there.

We didn't have any survey equipment, no measuring tapes were brought out. Paul, Scott, Matt and I just stood around, looking over our shoulders at the pine trees, occasionally kicking at a clump of sod, and gazing down on the grassy gully. Someone stabbed his shovel into the ground, someone else said, "Maybe start a square." I don't know if it made sense for it to be square because it was generally known that all the good holes were square, or if it was only because there were four of us, and each of us could take a corner. Maybe if there had only been three of us the hole would have taken on the shape of a triangle. That would have been a different hole.

We dug hard, we dug excitedly, we dug to get tired. We dug because digging is doing something and everybody has to do something—most of the struggle is figuring out what to do. We dug with an amazing fervour, and we dug even though we weren't exactly sure what the end was yet. Soon we had a good eight-by eight-foot hole started. The digging was easy in the sandy soil at the top of the gully, near the pines. We talked as we dug.

Every time someone hit a rock we would all gather around. We hadn't even been digging for anything, just digging, nevertheless we would gather all around, wondering what treasure we might possibly be unearthing, forgetting that when we started out there wasn't even any mention of treasure or of something that needed to be unearthed. You never knew though; a lot of rocks got a funny greeting, like the guy you waste the surprise on at a birthday party.

After hours of digging we all became hungry, but our work seemed so important and urgent that we couldn't all leave the hole. By this point we had dug the hole so deep that one needed help getting out of it. So we elected Scott to go foraging, and hoisted him out. Scott trotted off to see what he could find to eat. Paul, Matt and I continued to dig, but only half-heartedly so as to have a bit of a break ourselves. We took some time to inspect the pit, talk idly about it, amongst other things, until finally the talk turned back to Scott.

"What is taking Scott so long?" Matt asked, with full knowledge that all we could give him would be speculation.

"I don't know," I said.

"Who knows where he's gotten to?" Paul said, and then, after a pause, "That Winker sometimes, wouldn't know his ass from a hole in the ground."

"Ha, hole in the ground ..." Matt and I mumbled through our chuckling, hanging our heads to half hide how hard we were laughing, looking up to catch each other's eyes every once in a while before chuckling harder again. I wondered if Paul had thought of it earlier, us all standing in a hole in the ground and everything. We couldn't get enough of the hole in the ground joke. (Of course, it wasn't really true. Scott had deftly shown many times he knew exactly where his ass was, sometimes with a match and a blue angel for our amusement, up near the stove—although we all had done our share of those—or with his patented flying-farting-scissor-kick that never seemed to get old.)

We were still chuckling when Scott came back. He had his arms full with some rolls, crackers, a jar with some stuff to drink, and some cheese. In his mouth he had already stuffed over half a dozen soda crackers. When I saw him I quickly took it upon myself to relay the joke. It wouldn't have seemed right for Paul to use it again somehow. I don't know what it is, but when there is a new joke you can't say it twice without feeling uneasy, when there are people still there that heard it the first time. This is one of the unwritten rules.

"Jeez, you took so long we weren't sure if you knew your ass—let alone a snack—from a hole in the ground," I said, and Scott laughed so hard standing on the edge that he sent soda-cracker crumbs cascading from out of his mouth all over the rest of us down in the hole. I guess that evened things out for Scott, being the first guy who we had figured didn't know something from a hole in the ground—not that the target of the joke much mattered. Now that we all knew the joke, the rules of using it were relaxed and the rest of that afternoon we tossed it around quite freely. By the end of the day all of us had been accused of not knowing something or other from a hole in the ground.

It started to get close to suppertime. Scott went to the house to see if he could find some buckets or something. Time passed and Matt went to see what was taking Scott. Paul and I continued digging, we had found a good slow rhythm that was in sync with the law of diminishing returns. Every couple of minutes a small piece of the bank would give way and a waterfall of sand would flow down into the pit—just a shovelful or two.

"I can't even remember what we were digging," I said after a while.

"A hole," Paul said.

"Yeah," I said, and Paul just said, "I know …."

"I wonder where those guys have gotten to?"

"They must be having some food. Maybe Mom got home and cooked something," Paul said, and with that, we used the handles of our shovels to climb out of the hole, and walked towards the house through the grass, tired, but the good tired. We talked about supper, and we thought about days too far ahead to probably think about and the things we could do, like digging holes.

After supper we got a second wind, but by the time we got out there it had started getting dark. We went back for a lantern which somehow made the whole thing seem a little grizzly. If anyone had seen us I imagine they would have thought they had stumbled upon some unseemly scene. I remember at one point we all stopped digging at the same time. We looked up into the quiet night at the faint lantern light reflecting off some pine boughs. The sound of the soft wind going through those trees was so lonely: an undying sound, like it somehow knew we were only human and it had found us. After we stopped that once, we never really could get going again, so we packed it in.

After that we did not work on the hole too much—the feeling had gone, our ideas had brought us to other things. We did not know where to go with the hole. We still didn't know why we had started to dig it in the first place. Ideas had been tossed around, but nothing had been settled on. We worked on it a little bit here and there over the next few days, but more out of politeness to the hole than anything.

A couple months went by and mention of the hole had pretty well died away; new conversations gradually silted over and covered any talk of it. It was destined to become an old memory, something that would eventually be forgotten. Lesser things have been forgotten, and more important things too. One day when things were really blowing from the west, the wind brought Roland Porter up the driveway for a visit. It had been a year or two since he had visited last.

Ron came out to talk and at first we all just sort of hung around pretending to do menial tasks close by—kicking at a little anthill or pretending to inspect a dent in one of the Toyotas, so we could listen without really seeming to, all of us still being a little shy of adults, adult life and adult conversation, unsure if we wanted any part of that frontier yet or not. Those fears were silly with Roland, and pretty quickly, like the way you hold out your hand to a dog for him to sniff, Roland's warm, reminiscing words put us at ease and we relaxed, no longer needing to pretend to do anything other than what we were doing, and that was listening to him. And so we stood around on the lawn near the driveway, the young and the old looking down the valley acknowledging the same things: the same sky, the Model A out of sight in the gully, the rare old ' Toyota Corona behind the barn, the seats pulled out so the floor could be worked on. We talked for a while and then, out of nowhere (Roland often had to talk right out of nowhere about the past—you have to when people don't know the questions), Roland said, "A couple of gullies over there, facing southwest, I always thought there was the perfect spot to dig a hole or some sort of underground house. It just always struck me."

We all sort of looked at each other. We felt we knew where he meant. No one had said anything to Roland.

Roland had not known that we had been digging a hole, we hadn't been telling people—we asked Ron later and he said he hadn't. Some people, they'd dig a hole and they'd go out of their way to tell you, but we weren't like that. And Roland smiled as though he knew, but it was the sort of smile that didn't come from anyone telling him, he just knew things in a general sense. And I said, "Maybe there was a hole already there in a way."

And some just looked at me. It's not always easy for others to follow such thoughts, especially when just a bit of them comes to the surface like that.

"I don't know ..." I said, but I thought maybe Rolly did. I can't be sure though, he didn't say anything. But maybe those grassy hills somehow speak to you—maybe the whole place does, as some places do.

16 *Green Fields & Pink Skies*

The sky was pink that morning. Things like that hardly seem worthwhile mentioning at the time, but it's the sort of thing people recall as being obvious in hindsight. The signs of spring: the first chirp of a robin, the first sign of green on a tree—and then there were the fields.

Wars and conflicts, although often terrible, sometimes fulfill a need. Like if you're standing in a field with a rope in your hand, you just have the urge to pull against something, feel the weight of something on the other end—your muscles tight, mind occupied—your life suspended by this rope, this struggle, almost as though you'd die without it, fall into an oblivion. With the fields, we never really planned it; there was no date; it usually took us by surprise, a sudden uprising. If the weather was right and the mood struck him, Ron would offhandedly mention that the old dead grass in the field, standing dried-out and brown, could probably be burned down at some point, should probably be burned down.

Paul, Matt and I were sitting on the couch and chairs in the kitchen; we heard the footsteps of Ron walking in through the French doors from another part of the farmhouse. He stopped and looked into the mirror that hung next to the basement door and checked his beard.

We usually burned the large field where we played baseball, that was a few acres, the little piece by the pumphouse, that was another half an acre and the gully behind the house, that was another couple of acres.

"It looks like there's a little fire over by the wall," Matt said, looking out the bay window at the rock wall that used to be the foundation of a great barn—with crossbeams far larger than you'd ever see now—from Rolly Porter's day. I wondered if the barn had been wiped out by a fire. Canning had been wiped out by fire four times, in 1866, 1868, 1912 and 1938. The dates were on a sign down by the old Canning dockyard. The fires would rage from one end of the town to the other, but each time the town grew right back—like a tree you tried to get rid of, but whose roots you neglected to take out. The old barn wall was in the field where the pumphouse was. Paul and I looked and sure enough, Matt was right, small wisps of smoke were tendrilling up into the clear sky, which was cool but bright and promised warmth.

"It's Scotters," Ron told us. "I said we should get rid of some of that old grass and all those burdocks."

I wondered why he had not woken us and collected

us together to tell us the dead grass and burdocks were to be burned out, but I guess this was it, him telling us. This was not a house with a lot of structure, or some sort of coherent form of governance. Ron probably just thought out loud for a moment, knowing Scott was near. "Something should be done about all those burdocks." And now here he was, a little later, checking his beard in the kitchen mirror a moment, with a view out the window towards the burdocks.

Paul, Matt and I went outside and walked over to where the little fire was growing. Scott was nowhere to be seen. I heard a bit of a noise over by the barn and suggested we check there. We walked over, I looked in the door and there was Scott pulling the old body of a lawn mower out of a pile of junk. There was a clanking noise as the rest of the pile shifted; I could see that he already had gotten the gas jug out and had found a little propane torch. He had probably gotten sidetracked by a couple of things while he was in there, shuffling things around. Scott looked up to see what we were doing, but like he had been expecting us.

"You just left the fire going over there?" Matt said.

"I didn't figure it needed me," Scott said.

Without much more needing to be said we left to look at the fire again and Scott came with us, bringing the gas and the torch.

"Which way is the wind going?" Scott said.

"To the east I think," I replied.

"Well, we'll concentrate on lighting the fire over here then and the wind can blow it along...."

Everybody grabbed bunches of grass and anything we thought might burn, lit them in the little fire and then spread the fire from place to place. Sometimes someone would put a little gas on a burdock and it would go up real quick with a crackling. Soon things got exciting, the morning was no longer quiet and you knew the day was upon us. In places the fire was several feet high. We ran around lighting more fires, sometimes trying to circle another person in with fire, laughing when they had to jump through it. We lit the old Christmas tree and took turns jumping over that too. We roved like locusts. It all seemed so amazing, the life the blaze took on: consuming, dangerous and beautiful. That was fire.

We were still playing our games when we noticed the fire was starting to get a little out of control and was heading for the pumphouse and towards some trees and bushes that were not to be burned. Seconds before we had been all about reckless destruction, now we were all about responsibility—to save the pumphouse, like a damsel in distress. We had a mission.

I remember one time Ron put an old television out on top of the pumphouse and we all took shots at it with the rifle. I'm not sure, but I think Ron was making a statement. At the time we all simply liked firing the gun and hearing the pleasant shattering of glass, the sound of a thousand untuned high-pitched chimes at once. That sound that seems to grow less pleasant when you grow older, tire of destruction, actually own more things made of glass—and when you begin to have younger ones around who enjoy the sound of shattering glass more than you do. Back then we all still liked that sound though.

The fire was growing out of control, which was what we had hoped for. We were our own Pereaux Volunteer Fire Department, putting out all the fires in Pereaux, most of which we had to light ourselves in order to get any action. The flames were licking the edge of the pumphouse already. Ron came out and joined in; I think he knew he'd have to. Maybe he looked forward to it too. For a while there were no fathers or sons. We got some damp rags and started putting out the fire with those. As the rags hit the ground, they blew the ashes and soot into our faces so we looked like a bunch of raccoons. Scott was putting out the fire with an old sweatshirt that I was pretty sure I had seen Matt wearing not three days earlier. People were yelling to each other:

"You have it under control over there?"

"Yeah"

"You?"

"I could use a hand. Over on that corner it's getting away...." And people were glad to lend hands, glad to ask for hands to be lent, glad to unite in a cause. We all had a purpose—one that would not last, one that was short-sighted and destined to be over within the half hour—but for the time being that purpose resounded in us so strongly and clearly that nothing else mattered.

Just when Paul and I were starting to get matters under control in one area, I would see Scott lighting the grass over somewhere else. And that is how it went, always lighting the next fire before we were really ready for it. The whole thing was a frenzy.

I remember when it was finally finished. I had just

 stamped a small fire, stopping it just short of some small trees, and I looked out over the field. It seemed like a battleground, the white smoke hanging in the air like a thick morning fog, and I noticed other people were finishing up too, soot on their faces, black ash on their jeans, walking and smiling, congregating in the middle—for what I am not sure really, but I went too.

17 *Fargos, Salamander Girls, Probing Minds & Fires (A great story becomes bewilderingly short & possibly not so great)*

Sometimes you can feel your mind growing strong, strong in understanding, growing loftier—competing, like in the great skyscraper races of the fifties. I sometimes think like that—people walking around just hungry for building supplies. The world is a stockpile all about; you can gather it all in with your senses. You can take these pieces, shine them up, sometimes shape them slightly in secret, looking over your shoulder warily, faintly wishing you did not even see. Then you can put the pieces in place and console yourself with their symmetry. Of course, there are times when you walk about and wonder at other towers you see and you shake your head sadly at their monstrosities and warpings.

One time down by the pond near the bulrushes where the tadpoles hide, I saw a little child with a stick. Hunched down, the child looked into the crystal clear water with amazement, delightedly using the stick to stir up the bottom. The black mud was filled with the life of long before, now muddled in the water, swirling, suspended for a while; the child laid the stick down and walked away with a funny smile and a look in his eyes. When I walked down to the pond myself a water boatman with his two long oar-like legs made a couple strokes through the now almost clear water again—maybe for me, but probably not; the child was gone and already the water was quickly forgetting.

The Fargo truck was a noble old creature. Down on Luke's family's farm, Rand's Land, they had a lot of old trucks for hauling broccoli and cauliflower. Luke and the Rand clan lived down in Delhaven. There were dozens of them, most farmers and farmers at heart, all good ol' boys (and girls) who never minded making time to stand around and shoot the shit, tell a few jokes—those sing-songy drawls—the sort of manner that made just standing around talking, looking around at familiar things, maybe with a beer in your hand, really feel like living—made you glad you were from a place.

Luke was my age, but there'd be at least one Rand your age no matter who you were. There were always little stories and happenings to connect a person. We shared a fascination for the legends of the Native people: the idea of a oneness with nature, making do with what you had, the spirituality of everything, the crow, the trickster. We'd make tepees out in the woods. Luke's hair was straight and black and I was envious because he looked the part—mine was blond, almost white. Luke said that was all right, because some

Natives had light hair too, when they got old. It wasn't the same, but I appreciated Luke saying that.

I remember one time while walking along a farm road, near a field we rented out to the Rands, after all the workers had left, I found a bag still a quarter full of the colourful elastics they used to bind up the cauliflower to keep the sun off them. This was back at an age when elastics could still excite a boy. I was delighted at the find. I took the partly filled bag and put it in the barn; I never did do anything with it. Luke might understand that story. Years later we would just be two people on John Deeres passing each other with a nod, one mowing an orchard, the other tilling under a field next door. Lives cross.

Things are often confusing, people, events, coming and going. Little pieces can be tied in, but just little pieces and then we have to go from there. One of the Rands' trucks, it was said, was army surplus. That was the sort of thing that a boy without many years behind him would take a lot of pride in. In fact, your new identity would be the guy with the army surplus truck—possibly a truck that people would look to again if ever there was a demand. My young mind somehow became confused. Maybe Luke had told me how one of their old trucks was army surplus, from the war, only a few weeks earlier. Somehow the trucks and the stories got mixed around and I thought I had heard that our Fargo truck was army surplus. It made sense I thought. Something that big and powerful, something that loud, that old—it belonged in a war and looked as though it had been through one. I viewed it accordingly.

When you are young, stories and events must be told over and over. New information is sucked up and then gone, like water poured on desert sand; you know most of that water is down there somewhere, but the process must be repeated if anything will come of it. Anyhow, when Luke told me the story again it seemed all of a sudden we had two trucks from the war. Young boys sometimes being as bewildering as they are, it is hard to know if there were really any trucks around from the war, but that wasn't the point really. Sometimes wills and dreams mix up with reality; this only complicates things when reality is as boggling and questionable as it is. That was how we saw the world, through the eyes of a couple of boys who thought they knew of a couple of army surplus trucks, the ones their fathers owned. In a way we weren't much different than anyone else: everyone has their own way of seeing the world, it's hard to compare these ways of seeing. There is no harm in speculating on it, but it's foolish to claim you can.

As I grew older I learned the Fargo was a '65, so that meant it wasn't WWII or even Korea, but still, the roots were planted and the old truck kept a place in my heart. I keep everything I remember as a child; it seems the old memories are always swimming around in the back of your head. You may sometimes forget, but you never lose them. When something from my childhood turns up in the present I latch onto it and don't even realize why half the time—from the tune CBC Radio makes just before the news of the hour to the smell of lilacs in June and the sight of big yellow tiger butterflies. These were my earliest memories, the foundation of my little building.

The Fargo was red, and had four large headlamps as well as a couple orange lights across the front. It was gas, and the tank was behind the seat. It had a large set of dualies in the back with a tire size that would be hard to find anymore. They had retreads on them. It was a three-ton dump truck with a large wooden flatbed. The deck had been lengthened so it could handle more apple bins.

The years went by and when I understood things a little more my dad would have me help him work on it. This I enjoyed. It was not in the best shape. The body was a little ripe, the door, which on the inside looked like it belonged to a '57 Chevy, painted red and white, had to be lifted up on to close. We had given up trying to patch the holes in the exhaust system; less back pressure meant more power anyway. In the spring we would put in new brake lines where they were needed, and every year the clutch needed to be bled. Little things like the points in the alternator would need to be replaced, and I remember one year I fixed the horn, although some maybe wished I hadn't. I enjoyed working on the Fargo when we took it out of the barn in the spring. That was always a good day.

When I was still nowhere near the legal age to drive, my dad would let me take the Fargo out to the end of the road and around the farm after we had worked on it, to see if it was running all right or not. He would continue to work on his projects in the shop. He had full confidence that everything would be all right with me driving around—either that or he just didn't think about it much, or didn't realize I didn't have a licence. He would often call me by one of my other siblings' names and I wouldn't bother correcting him. I knew who he meant. He was notorious for forgetting and losing kids or letting them discover their own limits. I remember one time we thought the Fargo was working all right and I took it down the steep driveway so as to head onto the road to test it out. It turned out there was air in the brake line and I had no brakes. The pedal just sat there on the floor after I had pushed it once. I still like telling the story every once in a while. It was a good thing no one was coming, but if there had been, I figured that I could tear across the lawn or down into the swamp without too much trouble or damage. I don't always add that last part when I am telling that story. If I do tell that last part I tell it in the same way that an old man telling a gripping story might tell it—in a way that downplays the danger as though to lessen the tale, but in a way that lets you know the danger has been downplayed, so now the tale is somehow greater:

"I suppose I would have just pulled it down into the swamp and there wouldn't have been much matter...."

When I would go in for lunch after taking the Fargo for a test drive, my mom would always mention how loud the thing had sounded as I roared down the driveway and around. Then she'd remind me to take off my boots and leave them in the mud room. I loved the thought of my mom managing the food that kept us all alive, me roaring out the driveway, testing out the truck after having worked on it, my mom rushing to the window to see what her crazy son was up to, thinking to herself, 'There goes that old Fargo', or commenting on it if someone was near, sure that I would get into trouble. She knew I was smart, but she must have figured I had no sense in a way that a boy often exhibits, often their whole life. It made me grin to think of how it all played out.

When I would go in for lunch she would make me a sandwich. Me, her son, only a boy beginning to do man things, would walk over to the sink and try to get the grease off my hands. Almost every day she would have to remind me to dry my hands on the towel, not just wipe them on my pants. "Don't forget to dry your hands.... The towel's on the towel rack" (it was never anywhere else). I would head for the towel after her prompting as though in a trance, not saying a thing, like her words had just switched on the hand-drying switch in my brain, or as though I was some sort of machine that usually needed a bit of a kick in order to work right. When I was younger she would even have had to tell me to wash my hands. She would say, "Do you need to wash your hands?" Back then I didn't really believe there was much sense in washing one's hands unless there were huge globs of mud on them or something. I would always say in a feigned exasperated voice as I held up my hands to show her, "They're as clean as beans, Mom!" For some reason I would delight in the way the sentence made no sense. Everyone knows beans aren't particularly known for their cleanliness. Maybe this is partly where my mom got the idea that she still had to worry about me, having to be told everyday to wipe my hands on the towel. The truth is, I sort of liked my mom telling me to dry my hands on the towel; I don't think she minded reminding me either. When my dad would come in, a similar scene would play itself out. If no one told me to dry my hands on the towel, I would worry.

During one of those talks that families sometimes have, where the kids talk about the various possessions they most admire, and the parents sit and smile and think about how their own memories are affected by these same objects too, often telling stories that were told to them, maybe in the same way, I said, "The Fargo is a good old truck and is a nice thing to have," out of nowhere. This was the first time I had raised my voice in the conversation. Everyone felt this was a fine joke. Caught a little off guard I decided I better add that the old antique music box was nice too; it had been in the family for generations. It was in a carved wooden box; there was a little red jewel on the flywheel and when you cranked the box up it played the most intricate little songs, songs that seemed almost as old and beautiful as the peepers in the swamp, but with a sense of family and fragile humanity. I wondered if when my grandmother was still alive, as a child, her little hands had turned the crank so she could listen to the song as she sat on the big bed. The notes were high-pitched and metallically twangy and somehow the notes seemed a little off, but at the same time they seemed just right, like there was something human in not being perfect. Everyone nodded their heads at this item.

So the Fargo was a farm truck. That is what you first saw when you looked at it, but I guess there might be more, there is always more. It was mid-morning on a fine summer day. It was hot and the cicadas told me it was going to be hotter; in the distance over the road the landscape shimmered from the heat. I walked to the Fargo, which was parked at the top of the hill. A little moss had grown on the running boards. Thin lines of grass an inch tall had sprouted up on the deck in the parallel cracks between the boards—the seeds from last year's hay. I removed the rocks from under the tires, put there because of my lack of faith in the emergency brake. I could just imagine if the truck began to roll when no one was around: it would go crashing down the hill, through outbuildings and possibly through our farmhouse, white-walled and red-shingled, at the very bottom of the hill, which had managed to escape rogue Fargos and other disasters for over two hundred years. I stepped in and released the brake and I took the truck out of the lowest gear and into a higher one. I pushed in the clutch and, with a couple of metal groans, it began to move. The truck would have started with the battery, but I wanted to start it by coasting just because I could. Once I got a little speed up I let the clutch out again to engage the engine; the back wheels scraped the slate road for a moment as the truck started to move faster than the turning wheels. After a couple of strokes the engine fired right up. I took the sharp corner effortlessly and turned to the right near the spray shed. With a couple more turns I headed the truck up another road that went back over the hill towards the fields and orchards.

Roaring along the fields in the Fargo, I was just happy with all the noise I was in charge of, kicking up the dust behind me like a brown vapour trail from a jet. It was hot in the cab of the old truck. The heat didn't bother me, but I couldn't help, as I drove by the large spring-fed pond, thinking with a little envy of the water beetles and skippers playing around on the cool surface. I kept the windows open at all times, so a thin film of dirt covered the whole cab. It seemed like a clean kind of dirt though, I thought. As I approached the nursery I saw that my dad was out hoeing around the little trees, out there in the hot sun. He always seemed indefatigable; he was sixty and I thought he had more energy than me sometimes, a lot more energy than most people his age. One of my favourite salamander girls was out there talking to him. Talking to him about the salamanders she was studying on our farm. My dad was a great lover of nature and so it was known that he was open to such studies. I can't even remember what the girl's name was. When she would say it I would only hang onto it for a second. It was no good to me, and I would concentrate so hard on what else she was saying that it would slip by. Our relationship was more on the "Hey, how are you doin'? … not too bad" level. You didn't need a name for that; it seemed as though it would be too intimate. Whenever we did have a bit of a conversation, it would usually end with me saying, sort of quietly, to finish it off and escape, "Yeah, I always liked salamanders, anyways …." I never thought I had much to say. I was a person of few words; it seemed people talked idly faster than I could think. I had much to learn about the art of small talk. You had to have a little bag full of casual things to say always at the ready in your mind, things that could just be thrown out there, no thought involved. I never really have got the hang of it.

I drove by them expertly, I felt; I hoped my actions were louder than words. I gave the horn a honk and waved, but did not slow down, as though my business with the truck was too important, I can't remember what I was doing anymore. My father and the salamander girl looked and waved as I drove by, and I turned into a little woods road, wondering if their eyes still followed the sound. The road had trees on either side, mostly poplar, which were tall and thin and would often come down in a high wind. Poplar always seem to grow bigger than they are strong. There were also a couple of maple and wild apple. The canopy met above the road, so if you were to fly over, no road would you see. I was just beginning to enjoy the coolness of the woods, and the little birds I could hear over the engine (or maybe I just imagined the songs, unable to hear them, my mind filling in for what it knew should be), when I noticed the black smoke rolling up from under the hood. I hit the brakes and jumped out without even waiting for the truck to stop completely; I ran ahead, leaped up on the bumper and threw open the hood. A terminal had shorted and had caught the top of the battery on fire; the flames had spread to some grease on the engine. I had remembered one time seeing a Honda Civic drive by on the main road at Jer's house. I noticed it because it was loud and the engine sounded terribly sick. Fifteen minutes later we heard sirens and followed them down the road a couple of miles, and there was the Civic in the middle of the road completely in flames, a mother and her two children looking on, having lost the family car. The two kids looked on with excitement: money they did not understand, but fire somehow they did, money not being as instinctual or natural.... The mother was looking a little distraught, and she was telling her story to a fireman—the first of many who would hear it that day I am sure. With the passage of years terrible things become less terrible and stories more valuable. The money the car cost, I'm guessing, would some day not make a difference at all, and her two children would continue to grow.

As I watched my own fire my mind raced. Too bad there was no one there for small talk at the time, because I could have given them an earful. I glanced frantically towards the pond, but it was too far away and I didn't know what to carry the water in—plus water might not be good on the oil and grease, or on a hot engine. I jumped down off the bumper and stood there like a sprinter waiting for the pistol to go off, but unsure of which direction I was supposed to run in. I started slipping and spinning in the dirt as I tried to get back to the cab as quickly as possible. I almost ran clean by the door and would have if I had not reached out my arm and grabbed the handle on my way by. I was yanked back looking like an excited dog who didn't realize how short its leash was. My thoughts racing and blood pumping; even though the noisy truck was no longer running, I wouldn't have been able to tell you if the birds were singing or not right then. I opened the cab door and looked in. I saw a deer antler on the floor, which I had found some time before in an orchard, and a crowbar that seemed of little use to me right then. I saw my shirt on the seat so I grabbed it and ran back. An old shirt, but one my mom had washed for me on a Saturday at one time—that thought went through my mind too, but it passed and I began to beat at the fire. The grease and the flames made it doubtful as to whether the shirt would see another day, but the fire eventually got put out, and so the Fargo would. I was relieved that the excitement was all over, and my thoughts began to clear, at least a little, like muddied water in a pond. As I stood there surveying the engine and the battery, I eventually began to notice the birds singing above me in the trees again, high up in the canopy. They had probably never stopped.

I stood there for a moment going over what had just happened. The truck hadn't been hurt any. I'd saved it: the truck that I had always known, that I worked on like a grown man, the old war truck. The battery might even still be good, I thought. It'd need another terminal end where it shorted—that was blown all to hell; we usually had a few around the shop. I started walking back out the road the way I had come; relieved the truck was all right. I became a little philosophical in my good mood, wondering how things happened, how different days passed in different ways. I walked along one of the tire tracks, a hump of grass ran along the middle of the roadway. I was hoping the salamander girl would still be there out in the field. I thought now I might have something to say. Even my dad I looked forward to telling. There was no end to the people I wanted to impress, at seventeen.

I reached the sun and was relieved to see they were still there. I walked out of the shade of the trees and into the sun. I stepped out into the field. They hadn't noticed me yet. I pictured how it would be. They would see me, a lone figure in the distance, marching along. Maybe they would be unsure of what they were seeing in the shimmering heat waves; as I plodded closer they would realize, but wonder what it meant. I assumed a slow but methodical pace, as though the actions of the world around me could no longer serve to spur my pace or emotions. The sun felt good on my skin and I felt strong. I thought about the truck as I walked along, the confusions of youth, how I worked on it, kept it running, how I had fitted it with some new brake lines I had fashioned out of some copper tubing just a few weeks before—the way I worked on the engine but still had to be told to dry my hands. The old war Fargo, the pride of my youth. Like an old soldier I marched along. I felt much older than my seventeen years. When you are that young every year you live seems as long, and you think you have learned as much as you have in all the years that have preceded it. Seventeen years old, and already the world didn't shock me, like it did some, I humoured myself with thinking. There weren't too many pieces left to this puzzle, all neatly coming together, square edges. I thought about the way I had reacted to the fire. I already pictured myself going about the task of extinguishing the fire more calmly and collectedly than I really had—my eyes not so wide, calmly strolling back to the cab, maybe hearing the birds, stopping a second to appreciate them, getting my shirt, calmly but deliberately putting out the flames. The histories were already aging.

The pace and the action of the stride that I had

assumed was something that no longer had to be thought about, one foot after the other with no more thought or doubt than the earth had when it turned. Every once in a while my foot would kick through one of the furrows spraying dirt up, but it wouldn't alter my step a bit, as though the earth changed for me and not I for it. I thought about that too. Inside my thoughts raced; I hoped no one could see that. I was looking forward to telling my story. I wanted to tell the salamander girl, my dad, that frog sitting in the puddle in the wheel rut—anyone or anything with ears—about how the world was and how well I understood it. Not outright just like that, you couldn't, but through my actions—the slow walk—and through my words, in the context of a Fargo fire perhaps. I hoped they thought that my thoughts were as cool and deep as the Atlantic over on the horizon, where a gypsum boat glided out on the Minas Basin, where it would head for the Bay of Fundy, by the whirlpools of Cape Split. And from there a boat was connected to any shore in the world, from the busiest port to the most remote bay. You'd think the gypsum boat was sitting completely still unless you looked at it over a long period of time. I knew it wasn't still. I felt as though I had looked at the whole world for a long time. I saw a lot of things that moved and changed though you maybe didn't realize it; although I was still curiously poor at small talk. As I walked, the story of the Fargo and the fire danced around my mind ready to be let out, to be free. I thought the story would be the culmination of so many things, a flood after forty years of drought, or seventeen at least: a much-awaited masterpiece.

 As I got near, my dad looked up from his intermittent hoeing and talking, and the salamander girl was looking too. "What's up?" my dad said gruffly. I gave my head a slight, nonchalant nod to the side, towards the woods where the Fargo sat, with a straight face as though tired of betraying my emotions, or as though I no longer really had any, all emotions having levelled out into what you saw now, a once turbulent sea now old and calm, a jagged rocky mountain now only a hill. For a moment I pretended like nothing really all that important was up, but then—maybe a little too soon afterwards—I started in on my great epic story: the story of me, the Fargo and the fire, of fires and the story of my life, of the world, of my understanding, of my simple mastery. I tried to assume a tone of voice that implied that something like a Fargo fire was just the same sort of shit I dealt with every day, like I just assumed everybody had Fargo fires to deal with all the time because I was so accustomed to them, so accustomed to everything, and so I began, my speech a little faster than what I had been imagining, my voice a little higher and excited.

"I had just headed in the road for Block Thirteen and I got to the top of the pond, by the little stream. And then the old Fargo I … well I saw smoke rolling out from under the hood, there was a fire and I had to put it out, wi-with my shirt … and … well … I had just put new brake lines on it not long ago as you know …." I trailed off, mindlessly fingering the charred holes in my shirt, not really sure where to go from there, if anywhere. I was surprised that after only about seventeen seconds, my story was done—nothing much more that I could think to tell, or form into anything intelligible, anyway. So quickly I was back to having nothing to say to impress the salamander girl, my dad, the frogs in the pond, chirping. I think I forgot to enjoy it.

"I thought I heard you stop," was all my dad said, obviously much better at acting like there were Fargo fires every day than I was—probably had seen his share of Fargo fires and the like and so it wasn't an act. The salamander girl simply smiled. I had been able to sum the whole thing up in two or three sentences. I felt like I wanted to say more, but there was really no way to say hardly anything I wanted without being staggered. The other parts still danced around in my head; I had not realized that it was all but impossible to form some of those things into words, especially for a seventeen-year-old boy in the context of a Fargo fire. It made little sense anymore. I wondered if everyone had these feelings of great stories that resisted being told, the feeling that they could package what they saw around them, thinking it was theirs alone to give to each other, when they were really just living, really not a story to take stock of at all, only human, something that awed everyone from the inside. After I had come out with what I did, I wondered at why I thought there would be so much more: the part about the soldier and the old war truck, the confusion as a child, Luke off farming too, me slowly walking across the furrowed field, grandparents and great-grandparents who listened to tinny songs from little wooden music boxes, how I worked on the truck myself and how it was funny that my mom still had to remind me to dry my hands, how the sun was shining on my dark brown back and chest, a sign of how often I worked and how I took pride in that. Just a couple of sentences and she knew all I could really tell, this salamander girl, and to be honest all I really knew. The rest was unsure. I didn't know how to bring it all together, and still don't really. If I could have told the story justly it probably would have taken seventeen years, but there was no way I could, I had not made enough sense out of it when it was told to me. The story I had actually told was just seventeen seconds of words, full of spaces and holes, my voice sounding for a moment in the field near the pond and then quiet, dissipating into the trees, over the pond, taken by the breeze and gone.

I wondered what the salamander girl would think of the story, what parts she would add to it when she thought about the couple of sentences I had just blurted out in a hurry, maybe retold over a beer to her friends. I wondered what made her remarkable to me without her trying. Would she think of the heroics of my sticking around the burning battery when it could have blown up? Would she think of the way I slowly strolled across the field, the way I was in no rush to get there, no rush to tell them? I wondered if she had thought of that—or maybe it was something that didn't deserve much thought. I don't think it deserved hardly any thought. My dad wasn't much concerned, and gave the dirt around one of the little trees a couple of hacks with his hoe. I took the pause to stare at my shirt—staring without seeing, just thinking, resting my eyes on it. My mom would not be impressed, I thought; I looked at my hands. They had soot and dirt all over them. Even a child would know to wash them.

I looked at the salamander girl for a second as she talked to my dad about who the hell knows what now, and I wondered. As the salamander girl and my dad talked I stopped thinking of the story, of the way I had walked across the field. I felt stupid is what I felt, and I was glad I hadn't tried any harder to tell that untellable story—just make a fool out of myself. I listened to their words without listening; I stared out at the pond. I no longer knew who knew what anymore.

Eventually, with a little more conversation, ending on a topic that had nothing to do with Fargos or fires, the salamander girl started off, back to her car, back to the university. Maybe she would have a story to tell about a farm with a boy who had dust in his hair and a shirt charred full of holes in his hands. Maybe she was a better storyteller than me. With a little laugh as she walked away she said, "and see ya Harrison." My name in her voice sounding strange to my ears. The laugh was for the Fargo, the fire, the dust. With a little laugh of my own I said, "Bye," and lifted my shirt in a wave.

I told dad that after lunch I would go get one of the Cases and some tools and come back for the Fargo. He reminded me to get a chain and a clevis, just in case; we might have to tow. As I turned to go my dad said he would come down after he'd finished that row, and he went back to cutting up the earth around the little trees, the ocean calmer, mountains softer.

Luke, living a life of his own, probably out in a field too, somewhere, trying to make sense of it for himself, who knows. The sun was further in its track towards the west, almost overhead now, almost lunch. I'd have to wash my hands, my mom would probably have to remind me to dry them. I started on my walk along the fields, down towards the barn, listening to the snipping sound of the grasshoppers in the long grass, dragging my short shadow, and just taking more in than when my thoughts were racing, flying over all the things I felt but really didn't know, things you can't really know.

Afterword

Yeah ... no ... I know, I'm still here. I didn't feel right just walking away without saying another word—the last story being the end of it, and then me just taking off. I always hate that, when someone just walks away without saying a word, their head down, shaking it slightly, scuffing their feet as they go, like you're supposed to know what they're thinking—and sometimes you do, but you'd rather they lied a little to you with their words before they left, at least give you a moment of human awkwardness and some stumbling over of a couple of words like you know you're supposed to, so you can feel better about it afterwards, and not think about it so much, because you both tried. I tried to get across to you what I could. If you saw a little of yourself in my words, then we may even part on good terms—for that is what people really like, to find a little bit of themselves here and there; it's like finding a blaze on an otherwise unknown trail.

Why'd I do it? I wanted to talk, hear my own voice

 for a bit, see what came out. Hoping what swam in my head was sense. I wanted to show Nova Scotia, Pereaux, Hubbard Mountain, people, the world as I see it around me. It sure wasn't always great, but still—maybe I thought I owed it all something: the salamander girls, Sally the dog, the old Toyotas, the people.

And also, like most who write, I guess I hoped to include something that was myself; for that is what writers do it for, why they strive so hard I think, in hopes that they will include enough of themselves that their souls will haunt the pages even after they are gone or while they are not around. This I embarrassingly admit. The attempt, it may be laughable and off the mark—like a kid showing you a dog they made out of playdough and you guessing it to be a tree—but still, it's something to work on. You put a little thought into it, occupy yourself, and I guess the world needs both dogs and trees anyways.

Well, either everything has been said, or I'm just tired right now—probably tired. It's more tiring to do nothing but think than to do everything but think, and so this is it, don't feel like beating the bushes for things to say, which means this will be all. Sometimes the act of saying a thing means more than what is said. Yep, the day has been long. I'll go; I may.

Harrison Wright was born in Pereaux, Nova Scotia, and raised on his family's farm. He has a diverse background in engineering, physics and English. He currently works as an apple researcher at the Kentville Research Station, though he can often still be found tilling his family's fields in the lee of the North Mountain.

This is his first book.

Gaspereau Press acknowledges the support of the Canada Council for the Arts, the Nova Scotia Department of Tourism, Culture & Heritage and the Government of Canada through the Book Publishing Industry Development Program.

Typeset in Baskerville by Andrew Steeves and printed offset at Gaspereau Press.

1 3 5 4 2

Library & Archives Canada Cataloguing in Publication

Wright, Harrison, 1978–
Probing minds, salamander girls and a dog named Sally: a Hubbard Mountain memoir / Harrison Wright.

ISBN 1-55447-005-6

1. Wright, Harrison, 1978– Anecdotes. 2. Annapolis Valley (N.S.) – Anecdotes. 3. Annapolis Valley (N.S.) – Biography. I. Title.
FC2345.A4Z49 2005 C818'.603 C2005-900124-0

GASPEREAU PRESS PRINTERS & PUBLISHERS
47 CHURCH AVENUE, KENTVILLE, NOVA SCOTIA
CANADA B4N 2M7 WWW.GASPEREAU.COM